# BLACK CHILDREN IN THE PUBLIC CARE SYSTEM

RAVINDER BARN

B.T. Batsford Ltd · *London*
in association with
British Agencies for Adoption and Fostering

*For Gulzaar*

© Ravinder Barn 1993
First published 1993

Typeset by Latimer Trend & Company Ltd, Plymouth
and printed in Great Britain by
Redwood Books, Trowbridge, Wiltshire
for the publishers
B.T. Batsford Ltd
4 Fitzhardinge Street
London W1H 0AH

ISBN 0 7134 7136 0

A CIP catalogue record for this book is available from the British Library

# Contents

# Foreword

In a recent publication, Charles Husband, Professor of Social Policy at Bradford University, states that institutional racism 'occurs whenever individuals in carrying out the routine practices of their employment or institution produce outcomes which in their effect discriminate against members of black and minority ethnic groups. This form of discrimination is much more insidious than that which may be attributable to prejudice, and requires much more extensive initiatives in monitoring, training and institutional change if it is to be countered' (CCETSW 1991:53). A singular illustration of this phenomenon within the personal social services has been service provision to black children and families essentially by initially white managed services which over the past several decades have been largely immune from the reality of the United Kingdom's culturally, racially, ethnically, religiously and linguistically pluralist society.

In my submission to the enquiry into the death of the black child, Jasmine Beckford, who was in the care of Brent social services at the time of her murder, (1985), I outlined some of the research which looked at service provision to black people. These services were collectively characterized as demonstrating a lack of knowledge of the communities being serviced; a non-recognition that individuals from particular groups may have differing needs which demand appropriate responses; a 'colour blind' approach to service provision; lack of desire to explore the adequacy of their own service provision and racism.

The study undertaken by Ravinder Barn is a welcome addition to the slowly increasing literature of well-researched accounts of the experiences of black users of public services. The book seeks to examine the experiences of black children who were in the care of an inner-city local authority social services department in 1987, and specifically tracked how the authority exercised its statutory responsibilities in respect of 80 black and white children then recently admitted into care, incorporating interviews with key individuals including some of the children themselves. The study confirms many of the views strongly held by black and white professionals who have worked in the field over a number of years regarding the eroding impact of institutional racism on the quality of service provided to black users which impoverishes services to all customers—black and white. This is a particularly damning indictment when one bears in mind that the authority in question was at the time seen as one of the leading agencies advocating the rights, responsibilities and duties, of groups traditionally discriminated against by state bureacracies.

The research also offered glimpses of hope and opportunities for celebration when it found that concerted efforts were being made to place black children in black substitute families, who for one reason or another could not remain with their family of origin. The maintenance of regular contact between black children in care and their families of origin was encouraging. Residential settings were actively seeking to incorporate into their structures, processes and procedures an anti-racist and anti-discriminatory dimension.

I believe that in the past decade significant improvements have occurred in the provision of state social services to black consumers and that needs to be recognized. There is *still* a long way to go and that can only be achieved in partnership between all the key players revolving around what role is carved out and protected for the consumer.

There is no greater authority than the primacy of personal experience.

David Divine
Assistant Director
CCETSW

# List of figures and tables

## *Figures*

# *Tables*

# *Glossary of some terms and abbreviations used*

**Black**: The term Black is used to refer to individuals of African-Caribbean, Asian, West African, Turkish Cypriot and Mixed-Origin.

**Mixed-Origin**: Mixed-Origin is used to refer to individuals of mixed racial and cultural origins. In this study, the majority of such children had a White Indigenous mother and an African-Caribbean father.

**White**: While the study makes distinctions between White Indigenous and White European, the term White is used to refer to both these groups.

**White Indigenous**: The term White Indigenous includes those of English, Welsh, Scottish and Irish origin.

**White European**: The term White European refers to those who are themselves from countries in Europe or whose parents are European.

**Race**: The author perceives the term Race as an ideological construction. It is used here in the absence of a suitable alternative.

| | |
|---|---|
| **B** | Refers to Black |
| **W** | Refers to White |
| **H.V.** | Health Visitor |
| **G.P.** | General Practitioner |
| **S.W.** | Social Worker |
| **NSPCC** | National Society for the Prevention of Cruelty to Children |
| **Vol.Care** | Voluntary Care (under Section 2 of the 1980 Child Care Act). |

| | |
|---|---|
| **POSO/ICO** | Place of Safety Order/Interim Care Order |
| **Full CO** | Full Care Order |
| **1969 FLRA** | 1969 Family Law Reform Act |
| **1969 CYPA** | Children and Young Persons Act 1969 |
| **1973 MCA** | Matrimonial Causes Act 1973 |
| **1989 CA** | 1989 Children Act |
| **FF** | Foster Family |
| **O & A Centre** | Observation and Assessment Centre |
| **CH** | Children's Home |
| **CHE** | Children's Home with Education |
| **RN** | Residential Nursery |
| **HOT** | Home on Trial |
| **CO** | Care Order |
| **R & D** | Rights and Duties (under Section 3 of the 1980 Child Care Act). |

# Preface

This book is concerned with the situation of black children in the public care system. It does not adhere to the assumption that there is nothing wrong with the practice concerning white clients. It seeks to address the significance of race and racism in social work decision making. Although the general division is between black and white groups, differences between ethnic groups have been highlighted both quantitatively and qualitatively wherever relevant.

The study focuses upon the policies and practices of an inner-city Local Authority Social Services Department, hereafter known as the borough of Wenford. To maintain confidentiality and anonymity, names of individuals and places have been changed. The borough of Wenford was chosen for the purpose of examining positive anti-racist strategies and how these were being translated into practice. Wenford's progressive stance in these matters made it an ideal location for study.

The research study examines the care careers of a cohort of 564 children who were in the care of Wenford Social Services in 1987. It also incorporates qualitative findings based on a sub-group of 80 black and white children who had recently been admitted into care. Interviews with social workers, natural parents and children further help to elucidate the care histories of the sub-group children. Readers need to be aware that since the implementation of the 1989 Children Act, much of the child care terminology has changed. Although an effort is made to integrate the new terminology, some of the former key terms and references are employed due to their relevance to the study.

Chapter One begins with an evaluation of the main issues surrounding social work with black families and children. In Chapter Two, the methodological design of the study is outlined. The conceptual and methodological problems encountered in this research study are highlighted.

In Chapter Three, the empirical findings relating to the referral and admission of children in the cohort and the sub-group are explored. The sub-group findings are integrated into the statistical analysis to provide an understanding of the processes involved. The disproportionate representation of black children is clearly demonstrated. It is argued that lack of preventive work leads to black children being admitted into care much more quickly than white children. Issues concerning preventive work with black families, age, route of entry into care and change in legal status are considered both in quantitative and qualitative terms.

Chapter Four focuses upon the experiences of black children in institutional and family settings. The study offers new evidence to suggest that far from lingering in residential care, black children had a much better chance of being placed in foster families than white children. Also, with the adoption of the same race placement policy, there was a ready pool of black foster families in which black children could be placed. A sizeable group of black children were found to be placed in white foster families. The problems encountered by these children are discussed in this and in the following two chapters. Social workers' ambivalence to the same race placement policy in relation to Mixed-Origin children is also explored. The situation of 'marginalized' children, those of Asian and Turkish Cypriot origin placed in African-Caribbean families, is discussed in the context of departmental placement policy.

Chapter Five addresses the issues of rehabilitation and discharge. It is shown that although better links were maintained between black parents and children than white parents and children, black children were much less likely to be placed Home on Trial than white children. Both black and white children who left care were either withdrawn from voluntary care, or they had reached the age of 18 or 19 when they were no longer the responsibility of the social services. Social workers made little or no effort to plan for the rehabilitation of children. In the majority of cases, there was no contact between the social worker and the natural parents.

In Chapter Six, an attempt is made to consolidate the major findings of the study. The predicament of black children and families is discussed in the context of the whole care career process. The political and ideological structures of Social Services Departments, the professional ideologies of social workers and the institutional racism of society in general are explored to provide an understanding of the experiences of black and white child care careers. The constrained and difficult role of the black social worker is also discussed. It is maintained that due to the institutional and cultural racism embedded in bureaucratic organizations, and the contradictory position of the black worker in the hierarchical structure, positive change is limited and incremental.

The study concludes by highlighting the fresh findings of the research in the area of black child care careers. The implications of the findings are discussed in the context of the 1989 Children Act. It is argued that social services need to take account of such findings against the backdrop of the pernicious effects of race and racism. For the concept of partnership to become an equal opportunity exercise, it is essential for social services organizations and social workers to take cognizance of the internal and external reality of black people in Britain's extremely race conscious society. It is hoped that this book will be used constructively by those black and white individuals engaged in anti-racist, anti-discriminatory social work practice.

# Acknowledgements

I would like to thank parents, children and young people, social workers and social services area managers for their valuable contribution to this study. This book would not have been possible without their co-operation.

I would also like to acknowledge the help and assistance given to me by John Triseliotis, Juliet Cheetham, Ratna Dutt, John Solomos, Mark Johnson, David Divine, Paul Pal, Judith Wilkinson, and all my colleagues in the Department of Applied Social Studies at Royal Holloway College, University of London.

A special debt of gratitude is owed to Balbir, for being my sternest critic and greatest support.

# 1

# Introduction

The personal social services have witnessed many and varied changes in the last few decades. Changes in philosophy, ideology, legislation, managerial practices and organizational structures have dominated the scene in the drive for bureaucratic efficiency. However, recognition of Britain as a multi-racial, multi-cultural, and a highly race conscious society amidst all these changes has been slow in policy and in action.

The Commission for Racial Equality concluded in 1978 that the response of the Social Services Departments to the presence of black communities had been 'patchy, piecemeal, and lacking in strategy'. Subsequently, other writers have been stronger in their attack in implicating racism as a significant contributory factor hindering a positive outcome for the lives of black people (Divine 1983, Small 1984, Stubbs 1985, Ahmed 1986, Dominelli 1988).

Social Services Departments have been oblivious to the development of Britain's multi-cultural, multi-racial society. They have been slow in understanding the effects of racism upon the lives of black people. The framework within which much social work thinking has occurred and continues to occur is misguided by ideas of harmoniousness. Although the rhetoric has shifted to anti-racism, ideas of assimilation/integration which came into being in the 1950s have not completely withered away.

Notions of specialist provision have gone hand in hand with financial thinking where much has been made of the possibilities of Section 11 funding. Such funding, introduced in the 1966 Local Government Act and based upon cultural and linguistic difference, has invariably been used to boost departmental budgets and the 'special needs' of black people have taken a secondary place (Duffield 1985). The response of the personal social services to the needs and problems of black people has been dominated by eurocentric policies, practices and provision. Consequently the services provided have been inappropriate and inadequate (ADSS/CRE 1978, Husband

1

1980, Kaur 1985, CRE 1989). The role of institutional and individual racism in particular spheres of service provision has been covered elsewhere (Cheetham 1981, 1982, Denney and Ely 1986, Ahmed 1986, Dominelli 1988, Ahmad 1991).

## The personal social services and race

The eurocentric nature of policy, practice and provision in the personal social services has meant a lack of development of services for black people. The personal social services do not operate in a vacuum and are likely to be influenced by the pervading issues in wider society. This section addresses the emergence of race as a political and an ideological issue in British society and its implications for social work with black and ethnic minority communities.

## From assimilation to anti-racism

In 1981, Cheetham argued that the shape and scale of social services was influenced by views on best and most desirable model for race relations. During the 1950s and early 1960s it was widely assumed that a 'melting pot' situation would occur whereby racial differences would be mitigated. An assimilationist dream such as that formulated by the North American sociologist, Park (1913), was envisaged. It was widely thought that it was only a matter of time before the black 'immigrant' communities would adapt themselves to the norms of the host society and become incorporated into indigenous culture. This was thought to be inevitable, especially in view of previous immigrant groups as for example, the Irish, and the Poles. Moreover, the African-Caribbeans were thought to be already assimilated into British society particularly because they spoke the same language, wore the same clothes and worshipped the same God as the indigenous population. It was the Asians who had to be assimilated.

A study by Hyndman (1958) on the Family Welfare association concluded that black people were making good use of the services and that their problems were in many respects similar to those of the indigenous population. Since the ultimate goal was assimilation, the social services did not feel called upon to respond to the specific needs of black people. Indeed, the needs and problems of black people were

2

not even recognized as being different. The universalist nature of social service policy and provision, whereby everyone is treated in the same fashion led to a very poor service being offered to black people. It has been estimated that although black people in their contribution to the economy pay equal taxes, each white person receives at least 30 per cent more from the state than each black person (*Racism*, London Counter Information Services, 1976, p34, quoted in Simpkin 1979).

It has been argued that the assimilation process was not taking place mainly because of the strong religious and cultural traditions of the 'immigrant' communities (Cheetham 1981). Also, colour was an important factor. Cheetham states that the 'dark skins' of commonwealth immigrants makes them easily distinguishable from the white natives, and thus total assimilation is not possible. According to Cheetham, assimilation is now widely considered to be undesirable and impractical, undesirable because it is an assault on fundamental social traditions of ethnic minorities, and impractical because it ignores the fact of massive racial discrimination which would gravely militate against assimilation, even if it were desired by minorities.

However, Cheetham's view is somewhat misguided and has its roots in a liberalist interpretation. It has to be recognized that the 'immigrant' was regarded as being 'undesirable' and a 'problem' from the beginning, as blatantly manifested in immigration control legislation targeted specifically at black people. Thus full assimilation was never a realistic goal of the state. In the 1960s when facts of racial discrimination were being made public (PEP 1966), official thinking shifted to a philosophy of 'integration'. Roy Jenkins, in a speech in May 1966, emphasized the philosophy of integration in terms of 'equal opportunities accompanied by cultural diversity in an atmosphere of mutual tolerance'.

In order for the integration process to begin, it was considered important to enhance an understanding of black communities. The family/kinship systems, household organization, marital arrangements and child rearing practices of the black communities came under close scrutiny (Kent 1965, Fitzherbert 1967, Cheetham 1972, Triseliotis 1972). The black family structures came to be seen in pathological terms because they did not correspond to the idealized 'nuclear' family of western society. The 'arranged marriage' system of the Asians, and the allegedly 'weak' family structure of African-Caribbeans were heralded as the source of 'all problems' (Carby 1981, Lawrence 1981). Asian adolescents, especially girls, were seen as

3

being caught in a 'culture conflict'; the African-Caribbean parents were regarded as being too Victorian. Such views are still prevalent today and are used conveniently to justify lack of appropriate services by the service providers (Johnson 1986).

It appears that Roy Jenkins's 'atmosphere of mutual tolerance' has been unattainable. It has been argued that social workers found black cultural values to be incompatible with their duty to uphold individual rights and interests (Cheetham 1981). Kent (1965) argues that because of their own internalized values derived from the wider society and their professional training, social workers will not be able to implement client self-determination and be ethically neutral for this would maintain 'deviant' identities. She considers the main issue to be social control and legislation, and views the social worker as a social control agent, not simply for British culture but for the 'middle classes'. Kent recommends a policy of assimilation as the only viable solution.

In the last decade the notion of 'cultural pluralism' has emerged, with much vigour, in the field of social work. Roys (1988) asserts that this notion has not been difficult for the policy makers and practitioners to accept, since it can be viewed as consistent with the tradition in social work which advocates respect for individual differences. Thus it is argued that needs arising out of religious and cultural differences would be met by social services because of the latter's tradition of respect for individual differences. However, this respect for individual differences has to be reflected in appropriate and adequate service provision, of which there appears to be little evidence (ADSS/CRE 1978, Cheetham 1982, Dominelli 1988, CRE 1989, LGMB 1991).

While the conceptual models outlined above serve a useful purpose in providing an understanding of the historical situation, they create an illusion of progress and advancement. For example, it is commonly believed that thinking has shifted from ideas of assimilation and integration to cultural pluralism. This analysis introduced by Cheetham (1981) and espoused by subsequent writers (for example, Roys 1988) fails to conceptualize the position of social work as an agency of the state. It is rooted within the liberalist framework which asserts that the role of social work is to improve and better the lives of individuals.

Connelly (1985) believes that prior to the widespread inner-city disturbances of 1981, the attitude of the Social Services Departments was of a colour-blind nature. She argues that the situation has changed quite considerably since 1981, and points to the high number of black councillors (Fitzgerald, 1984) as evidence of this. Connelly adopts an unduly positive stance. The belief is clearly that great changes are taking place in the interests of the black community. Roys (1988), however, while acknowledging the year 1981 as a demarcation point, argues that despite the elevation of some black people in the political structure, the general picture looks rather bleak and black communities continue to get a raw deal.

While the above two accounts are conflicting in nature regarding the extent of changes which have taken place in the 1980s, they are both concerned with the latest developments in social services. In recent years there has been the emergence of a new approach in tackling the problems of black people. The race relations industry has witnessed a massive growth. The emphasis has shifted from cultural awareness to racism awareness. The need to employ black staff at all levels as well as the importance of appropriate services has been stressed (ADSS/CRE 1978, CRE 1989).

The response of the social services which have engaged in this process has been described as anti-racist. It is important to note that the anti-racist approach, as it is being employed in social services, is based on a number of assumptions. Firstly, it assumes that given the 'right' type of training, white social workers will be able to work with black clients. Secondly, it assumes that the employment of black social workers will, without any additional changes, be in the interests of black clients. Thirdly, it assumes that social services play a beneficial role and that if services could be made relevant for the needs of black people then they, like the indigenous population, would also reap the fruits of this welfare state society.

This type of anti-racist approach, like its predecessors, overlooks the coercive role of the state in the field of social work. Recommendations such as those made by the ADSS/CRE report in 1978 are being implemented at a highly incremental pace. It would be nothing short of complacency to assume that the response of the social services has moved along a continuum of race relations thought, that is, from assimilation in the 1950s to anti-racism in the 1980s and 1990s. As has been pointed out by Roys (1988) and more recently by a CRE report (1989), evidence suggests that only a small minority of local authorities have taken a positive anti-racist stance in their policy and provision.

It is clear that culture still forms the basis of much of social work thinking. Problems are perceived at an individual interpersonal level and needs are met accordingly. The continual use and misuse of Section 11 funding by local authorities is testimony to this (Duffield 1985). Since the very notion of Section 11 funding is based on cultural differences, local authorities making use of such money find it difficult to break out of the assimilation/integrationist mould. It has been argued that the major aim of such funding is to ensure that social and cultural differences of the 'New Commonwealth and Pakistan' communities are mitigated (Husband 1980). In the 1960s, Section 11 funding was introduced under the rubric that the problems and needs of black people were related to adjustment in a new society and therefore ephemeral in nature. There was little recognition of long-term difficulties. Continual use of specialist funding not only leads to marginalization but serves to reinforce the myth that the problems of black people are pathological.

Although the last decade has witnessed an increase in the employ-ment of black social workers, emphasis on racism awareness training and the introduction of equal opportunities, the overall picture is one of little change (CRE 1989). A lack of effective implementation of equal opportunities policies means that black workers continue to be marginalized, isolated and are politically ineffectual. Moreover, the 'deficit model' of the black family continues to be employed, resulting in poor service provision.

## Black children in care

Child care is an area of much concern in the personal social services. Policy practice and provision is essentially said to be directed to meet the interests of the child. In the last few decades much has been written on the subject of children in care. However, scant attention has been given to the situation of black children. To date, there has been no systematic research into the articulation and operationaliza-tion of the statutory care of black children.

In 1985, an HMSO report summarized the findings of nine DHSS funded studies in a report entitled 'Social Work Decisions in Child Care'. These studies explored the various aspects of the care career process (Packman et al 1986; Millham et al 1986; Vernon and Fruin 1985; Fisher et al 1986; Rowe et al 1984; Sinclair 1984; Hilgendorf

1981; Adcock et al 1983; Stevenson and Smith, unpublished). It is pertinent to point out that not one of these nine studies focused on the race dimension. This is perhaps also a reflection of the 'colour blind' approach which continues to exist in the personal social services.

## Entry into care

There are no national statistics on the number of black children in care. We know little about the circumstances under which black families come to the attention of the personal social services and their subsequent treatment by these agencies. In short, although much has been written about the care careers of white children, understanding of black children's care experiences is largely impressionistic and anecdotal.

Despite this flagrant neglect of the needs and concerns of black children, a review of the available literature suggests that concern, albeit misplaced, for the black child was expressed as long ago as 1954 in a paper entitled 'The Problem of the Coloured Child: The Experience of the National Children's Home' (NCH 1954).

Some research studies have focused on black children's admission into the care system. These have principally shown that black children are much more likely to come into care than white children. Foren and Batta (1970) showed that Mixed-Origin children were eight-and-a-half times more likely to come into care than White Indigenous children and African-Caribbean and Asian children. A subsequent study conducted in 1975 obtained similar findings (Batta, McCulloch and Smith 1975). Both studies revealed that children of Mixed-Origin came into care at an earlier age and tended to stay in care for longer periods. The second study also showed that the number of African-Caribbean and Asian children coming into care had increased much faster than the other two groups since the last study was done. Moreover, African-Caribbean and Asian children were found to be in care under care orders relating to offences. It was noted that one in every three of this group was in care for 'grave offences' as compared with only one in every ten of the Mixed-Origin and one in every five of the white children. The third Bradford study conducted in 1978 confirmed the findings of the earlier studies with regard to children of Mixed-Origin.

Other studies have indicated the high presence of black children in the care system. Rowe and Lambert (1973) in their study of substitute family placements in 28 agencies (county, borough, and voluntary bodies in England, Wales and Scotland) found that, in their sample group, one child in every five was black. They assert that the proportion of black children varied from none to over 50 per cent. Similarly, Lindsay Smith (1979) found figures of between 7 per cent in suburban areas and 50 per cent in some inner city areas. Two Social Services Departmental studies have documented the high presence of black children in their care (Lambeth 1981, Tower Hamlets 1982).

Whilst the high presence of black children in the public care system has been documented, there is very little reliable research evidence to suggest how and why black families come to be known to the social services, and under what circumstances black children enter care. Much of the evidence for the presence of black children in the care system is anecdotal and of a speculative nature (Ahmed 1981, Arnold 1982, Liverpool 1982, ABSWAP 1983). Explanations have ranged from socio-economic disadvantage to family background and institutional and individual racism on the part of the social services (Adams 1981, CARF 1983).

Previous research has also not concerned itself with providing an exploratory account of black children's care histories. There is no existing knowledge base available to address issues of black children's previous care episodes, legal status, age and gender.

## Experiences in care

As is the case with black children's admission into care, there is a paucity of information on black children's experiences in the care system. The research in this area is again limited and has primarily focused on substitute family settings, namely transracial placements.

A number of studies have documented the high representation of black children in residential institutions including CHEs (Community Home Schools with Education on the premises, formerly known as Approved Schools) (Lambert 1970, Rowe and Lambert 1973, Pearce 1974, Cawson 1977). A correlation is drawn between delinquency and CHE, although a definition of the term delinquency is unclear. Lambert (1970) in his study of Birmingham, for example, found that a number of Asian, African-Caribbean, and Mixed-Origin children ended up in CHEs simply because of some conflict between themselves and their parents. Pearce (1974) in his study of 125 Approved Schools concluded that African-Caribbean boys were 'over-represented in Community Home Schools, possibly as a result of differential police activity' (Pearce 1974:323).

The treatment of black children in residential institutions is a much neglected area. A CRE report (1979) stated that the basic needs (for example skin and hair care, and dietary needs) of black children were not being adequately met. This suggests that if the basic needs are left unmet, there is little likelihood of an overall satisfactory situation.

There have been assertions of institutional and individual racism in the residential care sector (Pinder 1983, BIC 1984). In the first ever national conference held for and by black children who were or had been in care, it was emphasized that children had been subject to overt acts of racism. Racist remarks from staff and other white children were not uncommon. It was also stressed that staff in these residential homes had little or no knowledge of the experiences of black people in this society or of black cultures, and therefore racial conflicts between children could not be amicably resolved. The lack of knowledge of black cultures and experiences was perceived to be the inevitable result of the negative stereotypes held by white staff. For example, when one young person asked about his culture he was told: 'You don't have to worry about that, you're in England now, and when in Rome . . .' (BIC 1984:24).

## Transracial placements

The term transracial refers to children being fostered or adopted by parents of a different racial origin to their own. In reality, in the context of Britain, it means the placement of black children within white foster or adoptive family units. The transracial placement of black children has raised considerable interest amongst academics, practitioners and policy makers. From the 1950s to the present day, arguments have ranged from the need for racial harmony to the importance of a family for a child regardless of racial background. In the last decade, other arguments pointing to the detrimental effects of transracial placements upon the racial identity of black children have gained ground (ABSWAP 1983, Divine 1983, BIC 1984, Small 1984). Recent studies into inter-country adoptions in the United

States paint a similarly bleak picture and warn of the severe damage to a child's racial and ethnic identity (Wilkinson 1985, Koh 1988).

In the 1950s and 1960s when the number of black children in care was on the increase, no initial concern was felt by the children's departments or the various adoption agencies regarding the placement of black children in family settings. This is indicative in the accumulation of black children in residential homes (NCH 1954, Gale 1963, Barnardos 1966). It has been argued that with the shortage of healthy white babies, many would-be adopters were prepared to consider 'non-white' children, and the practice of transracial placements became commonplace (Gill and Jackson 1983, Hall 1985, Divine 1985).

The practice of transracial placements thus began in the late 1960s as a solution to a problem – the problem of too many black children in institutional care needing substitute homes and the problem of there not being enough 'adoptable' white children in the same situation. The two complemented each other perfectly. The demographic realities fitted comfortably with the 1960s 'melting pot' philosophy of race relations which held that race was insignificant and integration was best achieved by mixing up the races. It is argued that many of the transracial adopters of the 1960s and 1970s were making a personal gesture towards a healthy, racially integrated society, and now feel angry, let-down and distressed by a different philosophy which challenges the basic assumption on which their racially mixed families were created (Hall 1985). The misguided notions of the integrationist philosophy failed to recognize the imbalance of power which culminated in the one way traffic of black children into white homes.

The three BAP studies conducted to monitor the transracial placements, all concluded the practice to be successful (Raynor 1969, Jackson 1976, Gill and Jackson 1983). Recently, Tizard and Phoenix (1989) have asserted that there is no conclusive evidence to suggest that transracial placements are psychologically damaging for black children. Unlike Wilkinson and Koh, mentioned above, they perceive identity in technical terms and fail to see a relationship between it and self-esteem. Indeed Tizard and Phoenix assert that: '. . . It may be that young black people can have negative feelings about their racial identity, and yet have a positive self-concept'. Thus they perceive racial identity and self-concept as two distinctly independent variables. Nick Banks (1992), an African-American Clinical Psychologist, questions this 'implausible' distinction. According to Banks, 'an integrated personality involves one having a stable concept of self as an individual as well as a group (Black) identity', whereby 'Black identity becomes an extension and indeed is part of the child's self-identity' (Banks 1992:21). It is clear that the eurocentric psychological perspectives require 'a significant perceptual shift to even begin to be relevant to considering the identity needs of black children and adolescents' (Banks 1992).

The eurocentric framework adopted by Gill and Jackson (1983) and Tizard (1977, 1989) believe that transracial placements are successful. However, at the same time they choose to pay lip service to the idea of same race placement. Divine (1983) and Aymer (1992) question this half-hearted commitment to same race placements. Aymer (1992) asks: 'Why should black people be encouraged and helped to come forward as adoptive or foster parents if the "other considerations in determining placement" can successfully be met by white substitute families?' (Aymer 1992:195).

Government legislation in the form of the 1989 Children Act which asks local authorities to consider the racial, cultural, religious and linguistic background of children is a step forward in the right direction. Although some local authorities have made enormous efforts to recruit black families with very positive results, there is a desperate need for a political will if this is to result in the appropriate placement of all black children. In the absence of more forceful legislation and the lack of specific guidelines in this area, there is a danger that the new act will make little difference to the existing 'colour-blindness' of the local authorities.


## Rehabilitation and discharge

There is a lack of literature in the area of rehabilitation and discharge. Research has failed to establish factors which might be influential in the rehabilitation of black children. While mainstream studies have focused on the situation of white children in this area (Millham et al 1986, Vernon and Fruin 1986), there is no similar information on black children.

Rowe and Lambert (1973) in their study of substitute family placements found that due to the difficulties in finding placements, black children were spending longer periods in care than were white children. This raises interesting questions concerning black children's length of stay in care.

In their evidence to the House of Commons, the Association of Black Social Workers and Allied Professions indicated that black children were less likely to be rehabilitated within a family (ABSWAP 1983). They found that in a sample of 100 children (50 black and 50 white) who came into care within the same period, after six months there were clear differences in their patterns of rehabilitation. In the white group, the proportion of children remaining in institutions was likely to be reduced by 60 per cent; while in the black group the proportion of children being rehabilitated into their natural or substitute families was greatly reduced. It is instructive to note that the definition of rehabilitation employed by ABSWAP refers to care as institutional care only. Thus those children who are placed with substitute families are seen as rehabilitated. A study conducted in 1987 explored the difficulties experienced by black young people leaving care (First Key 1987). While this study has raised our awareness of the problems faced by black youngsters in terms of employment and accommodation, it is unable to shed light on the rehabilitation and discharge aspects of care.

The rehabilitation and discharge of black children has been a much neglected area. Questions such as: at what age are black children generally discharged from care? what is their legal status in care? what links are maintained with the birth family/relatives when in care? and how important are these links in the eventual discharge of children? remain unanswered.

As a consequence of the issues highlighted on the situation of black children, concern at policy and practice level has been to combat the high proportion of black children in the care system. However, this concern has only manifested itself in the disposal of such children, that is, by finding substitute families for them. Research evidence in the 1960s and 1970s indicated that black children were over-represented in institutional care and were likely to spend longer periods in such establishments, due to the difficulty of finding substitute families (Gale 1963, Barnardos 1966, Lambert 1970, Rowe and Lambert 1973, Pearce 1974, Cawson 1977). In recent years, the negative effects of transracially-placed black children have also been voiced (ABSWAP 1983, Divine 1983, BIC 1984, Small 1984). The success of some of the campaigns to recruit black substitute families have proved that black children can be placed with black families

(Cheetham 1982, Arnold and James 1988). Local authorities have channelled their efforts in this direction. The fact that black children are admitted into care at a disproportionate rate has received little attention. The preoccupation of previous research with the numbers of black children in institutional settings and the problems of finding substitute families for them has dominated the debate concerning black children and public care.

In the light of the fact that very little is known of the care careers of black children, it is inconceivable that social services are equipped to make plans for these children. Also, it would appear that with a few exceptions, social services are still operating in a colour-blind fashion (CRE 1989).

## A guide to the book

This book examines the care careers of black children in an inner-city Local Authority Social Services Department. The gatekeeping role of field social workers in their work with families and children when children are admitted into local authority care is explored. An attempt is made to analyse the perceptions of the major characters – namely field social workers, parents and children.

The initial impetus for this research came from the growing debate about the increasing numbers of black children in local authority children's homes, and the increasing reluctance of some local authorities to continue to place black children in transracial family settings. An examination of the literature suggested that there were disproportionate numbers of black children in the public care system. Such disproportionate representation, however, had not been satisfactorily documented; although the difficulties of finding substitute families for black children had received some attention.

It appeared that while certain aspects of the care process had been examined, there was a lack of understanding of the total care career situation. For example, while impressionistic, anecdotal and some research evidence existed to suggest the disproportionate representation of black children, there was very little that was actually known to prove, describe or explain this phenomenon. Issues such as the circumstances under which black children enter care, their age, legal status, length of time in care, and previous care episodes were largely unexplored.

In order to understand the totality of the situation, rather than particular aspects of care, it was decided to focus upon the whole care career process. The primary hypothesis concerned the concept of race and child care careers. The study set out to explore whether race as a variable was an important factor in the process of a child's care career. This was to be operationalized by means of several observable indicators, for example, the differences in the patterns of referral, admission, placement and rehabilitation of black and white children; social work decision-making; and social workers' construction of reality/perceptions of race.

There was no sampling selection in the study. In the absence of information in the area of black child care careers, it was felt more appropriate to avoid restrictions of age, legal status, and placement. The care career of every child, whatever the route of entry into care, became the focus of the study. A cohort group of 564 children (294 black and 270 white) was found to be in the care of Wenford Social Services Department at the time of the research in 1987. The initial inquiry was followed up six months later to examine the change in circumstances focusing in particular on the process of rehabilitation and discharge.

The case histories of a sub-group of 80 children (who had been admitted into care within the previous six months) were examined in depth. Here, interviews with principal individuals (social workers, natural parents and children) were conducted to gain their perception of the situation. Both the cohort and the sub-group comprised children of all ages and all legal routes of entry.

# 2

# *Methodology*

Due to the paucity of information in this area, this study adopted an exploratory stance in examining the care careers of black children. The various issues stemming from the research design employed in this project are highlighted in this chapter. The research problem and the aims and objectives of this study are outlined in the context of the inevitable methodological limitations, and the particular problems encountered. The methodological conflicts and constraints in conducting anti-racist research are addressed in the light of the author's own experiences.

## Background to the research

The study was developed primarily at three levels:

1. A review of the mainstream, and race and child care literature.
2. Formulation of research designed to elicit information from case files, and from interviews with key individuals.
3. An examination of policy documents, and papers in the field of equal opportunities and anti-racism, and child care services and practice.

The shape and scale of this study arose from an analysis of the secondary sources. A review of the literature led to a model of research which focused not only on the recipients of the service but also upon the policies and practices of the service providing organization. An examination of the power dynamics between the bureaucratic organization and the service users was considered to be vital. Moreover, it was felt that the focus on the lives of families, both black and white, should not be from a problematic stance as had invariably been the case hitherto, but from an exploratory perspective.

The previous chapter drew attention to the serious lack of information in the area of race and the public care system. Little attention has been given to the care careers of black children (Barn 1990). Much of the literature has concerned itself with the high proportions of black children in care without adequately exploring the issues behind their high presence. Since most research conducted in this area has been of a 'problem oriented' nature, little light has been shed on the circumstances by which black children come to be represented in the care system.

In the absence of national and local statistics on the racial origin of children in care, some of the research studies have been preoccupied with documenting the disproportionate representation of black children without much explanation as to why they are there (Foren and Batta 1969, Lambert 1970, Rowe and Lambert 1973, McCulloch, Batta and Smith 1979, Batta and Mawby 1981, Boss and Homeshaw 1975, Lambeth 1981, Tower Hamlets 1982). Attempts to offer explanations for the large number of black children in the care system have invariably been located within the black family (Fitzherbert 1967, McCulloch, Batta and Smith 1979).

The power balance manifested in these studies has been particularly noticeable. Most research studies have immersed themselves in explorations of black family structures and lifestyles, leading some commentators to assert that the black family has been pathologized (Carby 1982, Lawrence 1981). In a climate of increasing studies in 'ethnicity', Sivanandan (1983) asserted that 'just to learn about other people's culture is not to learn about the racism of one's own' (Sivanandan 1983:5). In the North American context, Stokely Carmichael (1968) urged psychologists to 'stop investigating and examining people of colour', and instead, to 'investigate and examine their own corrupt society' (Carmichael 1968:174).

Johnson (1986) has pointed to the paradoxical use of racial stereotypes by service agencies. He asserts that on the one hand such stereotypes are convenient when justifying the non-existence of appropriate service provision, however they come in to conflict with the pathological notions of the black family – 'that migrant families are incapable of fending for themselves, make poor adoptive parents and require more intervention than "normal families"' (Johnson 1986:85). It is pertinent to note that whilst black family structures have been placed under the microscope, the practices of social service agencies have never been examined in a similar fashion. The number-crunching/problem-centred approach has done an enormous disservice to black communities.

Some research studies such as those by Pinder and Shaw (1974), and Adams (Lambeth 1981) have focused on the service providers, albeit in a limited way. These studies have attempted to explore the perceptions of white social workers and compare these with the perceptions of service users. The framework within which they have developed their analysis has been the orthodox class system model. This has meant that the researchers have failed to incorporate and emphasize issues of race, ethnicity, culture and religion explicitly into their methodologies. The Wenford study attempted to consolidate not only issues of class and socio-economic disadvantage but specifically, to integrate race, ethnicity, culture and religion into the research framework. The shift in focus to examine social work practice in a powerful bureaucratic organization became the central underlying theme to conceptualize the dynamics of the situation. Thus social work decision- making became as much the concern of this study as an exploration of the circumstances of the families and children.

Obtaining access to social services to conduct this research was fraught with difficulties. Bureaucratic organizations wield a tremendous amount of power, at times operating exclusively as insular systems. When issues of race and ethnicity in the context of anti-racist research are added to the equation, bureaucratic power, insularity and parochialism become very clearly defined. The power of social workers and managers is exemplified in the vigorous attempts made to prevent the research being conducted at all cost. Arguments such as: this piece of work will be 'too demanding of our time', the research design is 'too ambitious' and the perennial reorganizations of departmental structures, are put forward in the guise of valid rationalizations. These serve to create the illusion that the department is dearly committed to research and evaluation, but the present is a bad time.

Bureaucratic attempts to mould the research design were resisted by the author, which ultimately resulted in the refusal of access to two social services departments. Bureaucratic power was wielded in the guise of rational arguments to prevent this research from being carried out. It is doubtful whether a modification of the research design would have resulted in access, unless of course the modification meant exploring the lives of black families to explain the presence of black children in the care system (Barn 1992).

## *Methodology*

The research was based on a combination of qualitative and quantitative methods which include the following:

- Pre-coded questionnaire for a documentary analysis of case files and reports.
- Quantitative analysis of relevant statistics.
- Semi-structured in-depth interviews.
- Participant observation.
- Department records/documents related to child care policies, practices and provision.

## *Pilot study*

It is almost inevitable that difficulties and problems arise with respect to methodological issues (Smith 1975). In this study, it was felt necessary to pre-test the research design.

The pilot stage allows one to test not only the pre-coded, and interview questions, but also to evaluate the feasibility of the study. For example, the number of possible categories to any pre-coded questions may need to be extended or restricted. Some questions may be rendered unusable.

The disorganized and incomplete nature of social work case files highlighted by other studies was also brought to my attention at the pilot stage (Packman 1986, Fisher et al 1986, Challis 1987). The various gaps in knowledge suggested that it would be a considerable task to record accurate information. Tracing the ethnic origin of clients and staff proved to be quite a challenge. There were occasions when it was necessary to read the entire file to determine this information. The following are examples of the indirect references to ethnic origin found in social enquiry reports, case conference notes and assessment reports:.

'X's mother is an attractive blonde.'
'As well as being physically handicapped, X is also a child of mixed-race'.

References to black children's ethnicity were invariably negative. Such negative conceptions were social workers' construction of reality, where the race and ethnicity of a black child was couched in a long list of undesirable characteristics. Due to their own everyday

18

experiences of racism, black researchers can be particularly attuned to the ways in which racist remarks are made verbally and in writing by social workers (both consciously and unconsciously). What is striking in reading the case files and in interviews with social workers is that there is an enormous veneration of the white nuclear family and the dichotomy of the good and bad parent is continually reinforced. Views such as 'this Asian woman speaks no English, and would be detrimental to the children's progress' were not isolated, examples. Social workers' decision-making in the process of assessment and intervention was much influenced by such ideological thinking.

There were numerous examples of cases where the information had either been recorded inaccurately or had not been updated. These included the placement movements of children, as well as legal status and discharge from care. Cases of children who had been discharged from care upon reaching the age of 18 or 19, and yet according to the administrative records were still in care were common in all four area offices. Team clerks, as administrative workers, blamed social workers for not informing them of the changes. Social workers, on the other hand, did not always feel the administrative urgency of the team clerks.

The files contained very little information on fathers. This was obviously a reflection of the mother's role in the care of children as well as the fact that the vast majority of children were from mother-headed single parent families. Such omissions are also an indictment of social work investigations. Interviews with mothers revealed that there were fathers who were in touch with their children and yet social workers knew very little of their existence.

Language, frame of reference, and conceptual level of questions are important issues of consideration in the designing of the question-naires for the interviews. It was possible to pre-test the interview questions with student social workers and colleagues who did not form part of the actual study. Appropriate modifications were made based upon the comments and criticisms of these individuals.

## Research design

The research was conducted at two levels. Firstly, a census survey was carried out of all children in the care of Wenford Social Services Department. Secondly, a sub-group of 80 children was drawn from the cohort for the second level of investigation. The latter consisted of children who had come into care in the previous six months. A follow-up study of the cohort and sub-group was conducted six months after the initial inquiry to monitor progress and development.

## (a) Census study

Smith (1975) points to the problem of accessibility both of samples and of the whole population. He argues that a population is only accessible if it can be identified, and it can only be identified if it is first defined.

Definition → Identification → Accessibility

Defining a population generally refers to the inclusion and/or exclusion of individuals from sampled groups. In this study, there were no samples of any type. Since it was a census study, there were no exclusions. The census study was free from sampling error, and it provided systematic control, because the same subjects were studied throughout the care career process. This consistency in the subject of study meant that empirical generalizations could be made with greater freedom and accuracy.

Information for this part of the study was obtained from social work case files by means of pre-coded questionnaires. The questions covered the whole process of the care career from referral to discharge. A 15 page questionnaire containing 35 questions on the care career patterns was employed. Questions ranged from examining the socio-economic background of the family to circumstances leading to admission, placement, and rehabilitation and discharge. Variables such as age, gender, and ethnicity formed the central thread of the research study.

In the light of the shortcomings of previous research studies, and the methodological restrictions imposed on sampling methods, the research was conducted in such a way that the total situation could be conceptualizeed with greater precision. Since this seemed an enormous task, it was felt desirable to restrict the research to a few area teams. However, because of the wish to explore the boroughwide situation, and for reasons of validity, it was decided to examine the situation of every child in the care of Wenford Social Services Department. Fortunately, the pilot study provided evidence that despite the disorganized nature of social work case files, the recording

*Figure 2.1   Ethnic origin of children in care*

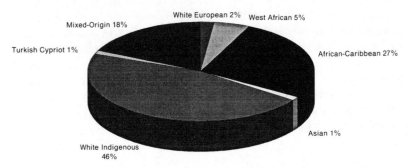

of information on pre-coded questionnaires although cumbersome was not such a lengthy task. The department's own figures showed that there were about 700 children in its care. The experience gained from the pilot study showed that it was possible to examine 30 files in a week, and thereby 120 files in a month. This meant that the initial census study could be completed within six months.

The cohort group consisted of children who were found to be in care, at the time of the study, in the early part of 1987. Children of both sexes, all ages, all legal routes of entry, and all ethnic groups were represented. The cohort comprised 564 children. Figure 2.1 above shows the distribution of children in care by ethnic origin.

Although seven ethnic origin categories were used in the original questionnaire, the findings of the study have been racially grouped as black and white.The black group consists of African-Caribbeans, Asians, West Africans, Mixed-Origin and those of Turkish Cypriot origin. The white group includes those of White Indigenous and White European origin. It is important to note that ethnicity distinctions are made wherever relevant.

It should be stated that the two categories white and black were employed because the objective of the research was to establish whether there were differences in the treatment of black and white families and children. Also, in terms of the analysis of data, it was simpler to group the black children together in order to draw comparisons with white children. Distinctions are made within the black group to illustrate certain processes which only affect particular groups of children. The number of White European children was insignificant and it was felt more appropriate to group them with the White Indigenous children.

21

A conscious decision was made to examine gender aspects. In the light of previous neglect in this area, it was deemed essential to incorporate sex similarities and/or differences. Basic recording of gender on pre-coded questionnaires provided a great deal of information when analysed in relation to other variables of the research such as age, legal route of entry, reason for admission, and type of placement. A higher proportion of black girls was found to be in care than black boys (53 per cent girls compared to 47 per cent boys). In the white group, there were more boys than girls (57 per cent boys compared to 43 per cent girls).

## (b) Sub-group study

The cohort study produced considerable quantitative data, however it required a phenomenological perspective. This was done by means of an ethnographic account at the sub-group level. The primary focus here was to establish the perceptions of the main individuals associated with the care process, so their interpretation and understanding of the situation was considered vital to the study.

The sub-group consisted of 80 children of all backgrounds who had come into care in the previous six months. There was no random selection. The only criterion applied was that the child must have been admitted into care in the previous six months. Events do not always remain fresh in the minds of individuals. The passage of time can lead to different interpretations and perceptions (Fisher et al 1986). Thus by choosing to look at recent cases, it was hoped that more accurate and reliable information could be obtained.

It was not possible to select equal numbers of children from different ethnic groups. The selection was wholly contingent upon the population being admitted into care. The situation was such that greater numbers of black children than white children were being admitted into care. Consequently more black children are represented in the sub-group. In total there were 80 children who comprised the sub-group, 55 of these were black and 25 were white. The black group consisted largely of African-Caribbean and Mixed-Origin children (28 and 20 respectively). Children from other ethnic backgrounds were in a minority. There were four West Africans, two Asians, and a Turkish child. The number of boys in the sub-group was only slightly higher than girls (43 boys and 37 girls)

## In-depth interviews

### (a) Social workers

Interviews were conducted with 40 field social workers who were the key workers for the children in the sub-group. There were roughly equal numbers of social workers from each area office, except in Area 4 from which there were only seven social workers. This reflects the lower number of children in the sub-group from Area 4. By mere chance, equal numbers of both black and white social workers were represented in the sub-group. This was the situation boroughwide and is not representative of each area office, which did not have equal numbers of black and white social workers. Area 3 had the highest number of white social workers dealing with child care cases; 50 per cent of the white social workers in the sub-group were from this area office compared with only 15 per cent of the black social workers. Most of the black social workers were from Areas 1 and 2 (30 per cent and 40 per cent respectively). In Areas 3 and 4, white social workers were more likely to be dealing with black cases. However, in Areas 1 and 2, a majority of the black children had a black social worker.

### (b) Natural parents

A total of 31 families was interviewed. Most parents were contacted by letter following permission from the social worker. Only three parents refused after a letter was sent to them. Considering the sensitive nature of the case (child sexual abuse/child abuse), a refusal was understandable in the circumstances. There were some parents who were not invited to participate in the research. In these instances, the social workers dealing with the case had considered it inadvisable to approach the family.

Of the parents interviewed, 13 were white and 18 were black. Black parents constituted African-Caribbean (15), West African (2) and Asian (1). It should be noted that some of the parents in the white category were parents of Mixed-Origin children. In the sub-group, there were 20 Mixed-Origin children; 13 of these children had a white mother. Four of these mothers were interviewed in respect of six children. Thus although in total, 13 white mothers were interviewed, 4 of these mothers were of Mixed-Origin children.

Many studies identify the client as one individual even when the work being studied is between social work and the family (Thoburn

1980, Mayer and Timms 1970). That individual is almost invariably the mother. This research study has confirmed that the vast majority of client respondents were women. Indeed, all respondents were mothers except in three situations where both mother and natural father/step-father or cohabitee were interviewed.

## (c) Children

Forty per cent of the children in the sub-group (32) were under the age of five, about a fifth were between the ages of six to nine and the remainder (33) were over the age of ten. Of the latter, 22 were black and 11 were white. These children were eligible for the sub-group inquiry. Only children over the age of ten were interviewed. For research purposes, it was felt that only children of this age group could best conceptualize their predicament and provide adequate accounts. Interview methods would not have been appropriate to explore the perceptions of younger children. A total of 21 children were interviewed (15 black and 6 white). There were 12 children over the age of ten who could not be interviewed because either the social worker considered it unwise or it was very difficult to trace them. Most of the children interviewed were black children (15). Within the black category, there were seven African-Caribbean children, six Mixed-Origin children and two West African children. Although there was one adolescent Asian girl who could have been interviewed, her movements between placements meant that she was impossible to trace.

## Data analysis

### (a) Cohort study

For the quantitative data, the computer software package SPSSx was employed to analyse the information. This began as soon as work was completed in the first area office.

There were a number of considerations which had to be borne in mind at this level of analysis. For example, a recognition of the limitations of statistics and the fact that they should be treated with caution and should not be assumed to be an accurate picture of any event was crucial. Moreover, issues of bias such as the errors in processing and statistical analysis, and faulty interpretation of the results made the author cautious to analyse and re-analyse the data, and to check the 'statistical' picture with a knowledge of process.

## (b) Sub-group study

All interviews with social workers, and most interviews with parents and children, were tape-recorded with their consent. The transcription of interviews began during the field work stage. Also, after each interview, any major points were taped immediately. These formed the guidelines for further analysis. Each interview was transcribed within days of being conducted, while it was still fresh in the researcher's mind, so that any distortions in the sound did not present too many difficulties. It was important to avoid an accumulation of interviews which would all need to be transcribed at once. When the transcripts were completed and analysed, themes began to emerge. The responses of social workers, parents and children were compared to establish differences and similarities in perception.

The preliminary research findings were presented at several educational establishments, particularly on the Social Work Course at Middlesex University and in the Department of Applied Social Studies at the University of Warwick. This proved to be a useful exercise in further analysis and re-analysis.

## *Methodological problems and limitations*

In interviews with respondents, personal characteristics of researchers such as race, gender, and age play an important role. Labov (1977) in his study on patterns of speech found that black children were far more verbal and forthcoming when interviewed by black interviewers, particularly ones who dressed in a casual style and who could speak the same dialect as the children. The use of non-verbal and para-verbal language (eye contact, nodding of head, and tone of voice) is also an important factor in the types of responses obtained. Many social scientists have asserted that good counselling skills such as those postulated by Rogers (1942) are important characteristics of a good interviewer (Schofield 1969, Smith 1975, Adams and Priess 1960).

In the interviews conducted in this study it is likely that factors such as race, gender and age all affected the responses of the respondents. It is possible that both black and white social workers were not entirely honest in their responses to a black researcher, or felt that they had to answer in a particular way. The following unedited quote which is a reaction to Wenford's equal opportunities policies illustrates this point:

> *White Social Worker*: 'Yeah, yeah, yeah. I think it's an excellent idea really to keep the culture going. I think it's really important. What else. What else. I think it's really important'

Such an erratic response to an open-ended question on equal opportunities policies suggests feelings of uneasiness on part of the social worker when asked such a question by a black researcher. It was clear from the in-depth interviews that such workers were not competent in concealing their true convictions and perceptions. Social workers' tendency to engage unnecessarily in discourse on race and culture gave a reliable account of their decision making when working with black families and children.

Did black and white parents react differently to the author interviewing them? Since parents were in a different situation, that is, they did not feel as if they had to give 'appropriate' answers, their responses were less affected by characteristics such as race, and gender. Age, however did seem important to them. Also, the fact that the author was unmarried and had no children of her own led some parents to believe that their situation could not be totally understood. However, the author feels that this did not affect their response as they managed to convey their feelings without hesitation.

A standard format employed in the interview schedule ensured that possible bias was minimized. A checklist of points to be covered was drawn up, but respondents were not all asked the questions in the same order. The order was changed depending on the situation and the responses given, to produce a more coherent structure. Such an approach meant that the focus was kept consistent. All respondents were invited to provide any additional information which they deemed important. Thus they were not restricted by the questionnaire.

While all social workers who were invited participated in the research, it is possible that the restrictions imposed upon the selection of parents and children may have biased the results. The parent's sample was inevitably biased since not all parents were asked whether they wished to take part in the research. The reluctance of social workers to allow clients to be interviewed has been the experience of other researchers (Packman 1986, Fisher et al 1986). Access to clients was denied in instances where social workers felt it inadvisable for the family to be contacted or when social workers procrastinated waiting for the 'right' time to approach the family. Although there was a reasonable cross-section of parents, access to more parents would have further enriched the findings of this study.

A similar block to access was imposed in the case of interviews with children. Social workers felt that it was their job to protect the children, and that they could not allow an outsider to interview them. The author's criteria, whereby only children over the age of ten were selected for an interview also meant that there were probably children whose accounts and perceptions were ignored. It is likely that this would have happened even if the minimum age limit had been set at eight or some other cut-off point.

The respondents generally required a certain amount of information from the researcher such as the identity of the interviewer, the legitimacy of the research, the process by which they had been chosen for the interview and the protection which they might expect as respondents. Also, the interviewer needed to be explicit with respect to how the information would be used, disseminated, and published (Kahn and Cannell 1957). In the case of social workers, the information they sought was provided at the stage of negotiations. While all respondents were assured of confidentiality and anonymity, there were some social workers who felt that the department should be named. They argued that it would be helpful if people knew which department was being represented in the study.

While the social workers were aware of the legitimacy of the research, and the author's credentials, an official letter was sent to each parent, after permission from the key social worker. The letter very briefly introduced the research and requested an interview. It assured confidentiality and anonymity. A telephone number and address was provided for the parent to seek further information. Two mothers, in fact, did feel the need to contact the university; one because she did not want to be interviewed, and the other because she wanted to make an appointment to be interviewed.

In many cases, mothers knew that they stood to gain little by being interviewed. However, they felt that social services needed to be told of the experiences of parents. Some mothers were just glad to be able to tell their version of the events to an outsider. On occasion, some parents perceived the author to be a representative of the social services. Their initial fears were overcome by a re-affirmation of the neutrality of the research project.

## Conceptual problems

There were a number of areas which presented difficulties at a conceptual level. Concepts such as the family, parents' marital status and rehabilitation may seem straight forward but proved difficult when recording information from case files. Such conceptual problems were brought to light by the pilot study and modified appropriately.

### (a) What constitutes a family?

While most one-parent, nuclear families, extended families and re-constituted families were easier to distinguish, difficulties arose when a family did not conform to the conventional definition. For example, were two parents living separately but having equal access to child single parents, or should the child have been seen as having a nuclear family?

### (b) Parents' marital status

By recording the current marital status, it was not possible to reflect previous marital status. For example, there were individuals who were separated or divorced, but were now cohabiting with someone else.

### (c) Parental contact

Here, I was faced with the problem of not only what indicators should be used to denote 'contact' but also what should be seen as 'frequent' and 'infrequent'. It appeared that face to face contact could not be measured as the sole indicator. There were some parents and children who had limited face to face contact but a great degree of contact via letters and telephone. It was decided that all regular contact should be recorded. In terms of frequency, although some parents maintained weekly contact with their children, it was felt that any type of contact occuring at least once a month should be seen as frequent, and a few meetings in a year should be seen as infrequent. It was not difficult to discern where there was no contact at all. However, what was difficult to establish from the files (except in the case of legal termination to access) was how this contact had dissipated over time.

## (d) Rehabilitation

Since the focus of this study was the care career patterns of children, I had to establish firmly what I meant by the term rehabilitation. While the stages of referral, admission, placement and discharge were more straightforward, rehabilitation created confusion. For example, did rehabilitation into the natural family mean that the child was technically out of care, or did it mean that the child was still in the care of the local authority but placed in his/her own family? Also, should attempts made by social workers to rehabilitate the child into the family on previous occasions be measured as indicators of rehabilitation? Since my concern was with the whole process of care, I could not perceive a child who was rehabilitated, but still technically in care as having been discharged. Moreover, although I was concerned with the current care episode, I felt that I could not ignore previous rehabilitation attempts made by the social workers. Rehabilitation was then taken to mean what the social services referred to as 'Home on Trial'. It should be pointed out that this definition precludes failed attempts which did not lead to the stage of 'Home on Trial'. Due to the disorganized and incomplete nature of social work case files, it would not have been possible for me to establish accurately such attempts.

## (e) Mixed-Origin

Mixed-Origin, like other similar terms such as mixed-race and mixed-parentage signifies little of the child's ethnic background. Small (1986) argues that the term mixed-race is derogatory, confusing and inaccurate and therefore should not be used. Without offering a definition, he suggests that it would be more appropriate to use the term mixed-parentage. While agreeing with Small that the term mixed-race is derogatory, confusing and inaccurate, the author fails to see how the substitute term mixed-parentage is a better alternative. Does it not have similar connotations?

This study uses the term Mixed-Origin. If one were to abide by the rule of self-definition for this group of individuals, there would be no complications of terminology for most Mixed-Origin respondents, in this study, perceived themselves as black. The term Mixed-Origin was used for a number of reasons. Firstly, while recognizing that the majority of individuals of mixed liaisons perceive themselves to be black, it is important to make a distinction to observe differences, if any, in care career patterns as has been shown by other research (Foren and Batta 1970, Rowe and Lambert 1973, Bebbington and Miles 1989, Rowe et al 1989). Secondly, the terms mixed-race and mixed-parentage are inadequate because they are both as confusing as each other. Also, given that the concept of race is an ideological and social construction, the term mixed-race is misleading (Miles 1982). It is instructive to note that the author does not find the term Mixed-Origin to be satisfactory, however it is considered to be adequate for the purposes of this study.

It should be emphasized here that the majority of individuals, children, social workers and parents who are described as Mixed-Origin were from one particular type of liaison, that is, they had an African-Caribbean father and a White Indigenous mother.

## Conclusion

The Wenford research study encompassed anti-discriminatory issues in all aspects of its work. The focus of attention of the study was extended following a literature review in this area. Indeed, the need for this focus to be extended to include an examination of the Social Services Department, its organizational structures, policies, and practices became a central concern.

The paucity of information on the situation of black children, and the shortcomings of previous research led to the particular research design adopted in this study. A census survey of children found to be in the care of Wenford social services seemed to be the most appropriate method of observing the overall situation of black children in the care system. This was complemented by the sub-group method, whereby interviews with social workers, parents and children made it possible to explore their perceptions to provide a greater understanding of black children's care careers. The shift of focus to examine the processes which operate within social services was regarded to be crucial.

Issues of power and control were encountered not only in relation to access to social services departments but also when individual social workers attempted to prevent access to clients. In some cases, this was understandable, but the paternalistic nature of social workers towards their clients was particularly striking.

# 3

# *Entry into care*

This chapter focuses on the process of referral and admission of children into the public care system against a background of impressionistic and anecdotal understanding of the over-representation of black children in care. An examination of the multiplicity of factors associated with this aspect of a child's care career is made in the context of findings from the census and the sub-group study. The circumstances under which children enter care, paying particular attention to issues of ethnicity, age, gender and family background are observed in detail.

## *The cohort group*

The cohort group comprised a total of 564 children (294 black and 270 white). Almost all of the children were born in Britain. Thus, black children were not 'immigrant' children who had joined their parents after years of separation as was suggested by previous studies (Fitzherbert 1967, Pinder and Shaw 1974). Whilst the black children were themselves born in Britain, they were less likely to have both parents who were British born. It was found that 50 per cent of the black children had a mother who was British born, but only seven per cent had a British born father. It should be stressed that black children included Mixed-Origin children. Indeed, 35 per cent of the black group were Mixed-Origin children. Black children who had a British-born mother were on the whole Mixed-Origin children. These mothers were invariably White Indigenous. Children of Mixed-Origin were the second largest group in the black category, second only to African-Caribbean children who comprised 51 per cent of the black group. The other three groups in the black category as depicted in Figure 3.1 were West African (10 per cent), Asian (2 per cent), and Turkish Cypriot (2 per cent).

Many families in the cohort group had had previous involvement

*Figure 3.1   Ethnic breakdown of black children in care*

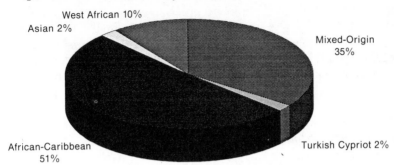

with social services (80 per cent). Moreover, about 50 per cent of the cohort had been in care on previous occasions. Only a small minority, however, had had several previous care episodes. No significant differences were found in numbers of previous care episodes between black and white children. Similarly, no significant differences were found between black and white children in the number of siblings who were in care or had been in care, or in terms of size of family (that is total number of siblings).

An overwhelming majority of the children (74 per cent) came from single parent families. These one-parent families were on the whole mother-headed units (89 per cent). The proportion of black children (83 per cent) coming from single-parent families was significantly higher than that of white children (64 per cent).

The majority of the cohort children were from families where the mother was between the age of 26–45 years, and the father was between the ages of 36–45 years.

Black children were much more likely to come from a higher socio-economic background. There were significantly more black children than white who came from families where both parents were either in skilled manual or white collar occupations. For example, 47 per cent of the black children had mothers in white collar and skilled-manual occupations compared with 22 per cent of white children ($\chi^2$ 16.982, p $<0.004$). It should be noted that these findings are based on 115 cases on which this level of information was available. Information on 191 cases shows that 63 per cent of the black children had fathers in skilled-manual and white-collar occupations compared to 38 per cent of the white children ($\chi^2$ 21.123, p $<0.000$).

The cohort findings show that an overwhelming (93 per cent) proportion of families were living in local authority housing. Black and white families were equally likely to be represented in this sector. It was not possible in this research study to collect quantitative data into the quality of housing, however research studies have shown that black applicants and tenants frequently receive poorer quality housing than white applicants and tenants (PSI 1984).

## The referral process

There are a number of ways by which families become known to the social services. These can range from families referring themselves for help and support, to agencies such as the school, the police and the health service.

It is important to note that about a fifth of the cohort were new referrals; whilst a staggering four-fifths had had some previous involvement with the social services. The Wenford research focused on the child's current care episode, details were therefore recorded on the referral which culminated in the child's most recent admission into care. Information such as the date, month and year of referral, the referral agency and the reasons for referral were observed.

## Referral agency

Previous mainstream research has suggested that parents are one of the major referral agencies (Millham et al 1986, Fisher et al 1986). In confirming these findings, the Wenford study shows that black parents are equally likely to refer themselves as white parents. It has been argued that due to their relative newness in a welfare society, black families are not familiar with the availability of service provision and thus do not present themselves to the social services (Kornreich et al 1973, Boss and Homeshaw 1974). The Wenford study found no evidence to support these findings in relation to parents of African-Caribbean, Mixed-Origin, and West African children. Asian children, however, were significantly under-represented. Figure 3.2 depicts the agency of referral for black and white families.

Overall, there were only slight differences between the proportions of black and white families referred by any one particular agency.

*Figure 3.2   Referral agency\* by race (%)*

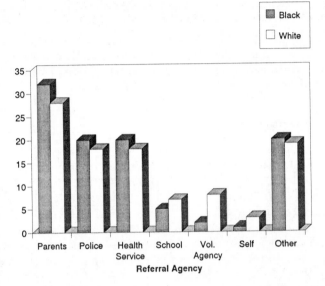

\*Referral agency here refers to the most recent referral in the child's care career, i.e. one which resulted in the current care episode.

Thus the proportion of black families referred by the police, the health service, neighbours, and parents themselves is only slightly higher than that of white families. One of the major differences in referral is one where a case is referred by a voluntary agency. It can be seen that while eight per cent of the white children were referred by a voluntary agency (usually the NSPCC), this was the case for only two per cent of the black children. The eurocentric nature of bodies such as the NSPCC is reflected in the low referral rate of black families.

## Reasons for referral

A multiplicity of reasons were found for which families had been referred to the social services. These ranged from the family's social relationships amongst members, to socio-economic difficulties and general neglect and abuse of children by parents.

Table 3.1 shows comprehensive cross tabulation of the race of the children and reasons for referral. In this table, the Pearson chi-square

Table 3.1  *Reasons for referral by race (%)*

| Reason for referral | Black | White | $\chi^2$ | p |
|---|---|---|---|---|
| Family relationships | 23 | 21 | 1.226 | <0.541 |
| Financial-material circumstances | 15 | 12 | 1.874 | <0.391 |
| Parental neglect/inadequacy | 22 | 33 | 8.644 | <0.003 |
| Failure to thrive/medical health/handicap | 1 | 6 | 9.195 | <0.010 |
| Mother's mental health | 11 | 5 | 8.458 | <0.014 |
| Mother's physical health | 5 | 6 | 1.471 | <0.479 |
| Homelessness-housing | 11 | 11 | 0.954 | <0.620 |
| Suspected child abuse | 11 | 14 | 1.115 | <0.290 |
| Suspected child sexual abuse | 3 | 4 | 0.021 | <0.883 |
| Delinquency | 6 | 7 | 0.509 | <0.475 |
| Non-school attendance | 2 | 6 | 5.882 | <0.015 |
| Child's behaviour | 7 | 13 | 4.964 | <0.025 |
| Other | 23 | 12 | 10.305 | <0.001 |
| (n) | 288 | 270 | | |

(n) refers to overall numbers in care. Actual percentages do not add up to 100 due to the multiplicity of reasons that could be recorded.

value and the corresponding probability values are given in columns three and four respectively for each of the 13 reasons. These probability levels indicate the significance levels of the race of the children and the specific referral reasons.

By choosing the cases for which the p-values are less than 0.05, six referral reasons which are highly significant can be identified. It is evident from the table that each of the six reasons affects the children (black and white) rather disproportionately compared with the remaining seven reasons.

The majority of both black and white referrals fall into three major categories, namely family relationships, financial/housing difficulties and parental neglect and inadequacy. Within these, the only significant difference between black and white group is found in the numbers referred for parental neglect and inadequacy. Children who fall into this category are those for whom concern had been raised by agencies such as the health service, schools and the police. More white families are referred for this reason than black families (33 per cent white compared to 22 per cent black, $p < 0.005$).

Other areas in which significantly more white families have been referred than black families are failure to thrive/medical health and handicap of child, non-school attendance and child's behaviour ($p < 0.05$). In the case of black families, mother's mental health and reasons categorized as 'other' are more salient. Black families are significantly more likely to be referred where mothers' mental health is an issue of concern (11 per cent black compared to 5 per cent white, $p < 0.014$). The category 'other' includes reasons such as parental substance misuse, disability, imprisonment, and death; and was often an additional factor to an already complex set of circumstances.

An analysis of the type of agency and reason for referral revealed some interesting findings. Although a greater proportion of white children was referred for reasons of parental neglect and inadequacy, and a failure to thrive; it was found that health visitors were twice as likely to refer black children for these reasons than white children (6 per cent of the white parental neglect/inadequacy referrals came from health visitors compared with 11 per cent of black, and 13 per cent of the white failure to thrive referrals came from health visitors compared with 25 per cent of black). Also, the health service and the police were much more likely to refer black mothers for reasons of mental health than white mothers (health service 23 per cent white compared to 41 per cent black; police 15 per cent white compared to 25 per cent black). The majority of the black delinquency referrals were made by the police and schools. Seventy-seven per cent of the black delinquency referrals came from the police compared with only 35 per cent of the white; whilst 12 per cent of the black delinquency referrals came from schools compared with only 5 per cent of the white. It was also found that schools were much more likely to refer black youngsters for non-school attendance than white youngsters (80 per cent of the black non-school attendance referrals came from the schools compared with only 38 per cent of the white referrals). White children were much more likely to be referred by their parents for reasons of delinquency and non-school attendance than black children. Thirty-five per cent of the white delinquency referrals came from white parents compared with only 6 per cent of black referrals, and 39 per cent of the white non-school attendance came from white parents compared with only 20 per cent of the black referrals).

## Reasons for admission

Most admissions into care occur at crisis point (Packman 1986, Fisher et al 1986), therefore one would expect to see very little difference between the reasons for referral and admission. However, since local authorities are under a duty to carry out preventive work to ameliorate problems and obviate the need for children to be admitted into care, one would also expect children to be less likely to be received into care for reasons such as financial and housing difficulties. The Wenford findings show that children were admitted into care where preventive strategies could have been attempted or were attempted but failed. Table 3.2 shows interesting differences between the admission of black and white children. It should be noted that in most admissions there was normally more than one factor involved. For example, child abuse was almost invariably associated with parental neglect and inadequacy, while juvenile delinquency, non-school attendance, child's behaviour and often family relationships went hand in hand.

The two most common factors in admissions were family relationships and parental neglect and inadequacy. Where family relationships were the contributory factor, black and white children were equally likely to be admitted into care. In the situation where parents were found to have neglected their children, greater proportions of white than black children were admitted into care (42 per cent white compared to 34 per cent black, $p < 0.037$).

In terms of gender, it was found that while similar proportions of black and white girls had been admitted into care for child abuse and child sexual abuse, significantly lesser proportions of black boys than white boys had been admitted into care for such reasons. Overall,

*Table 3.2  Reasons for admission by race (%)*

| Reason for referral | Black | White | $\chi^2$ | p |
|---|---|---|---|---|
| Family relationships | 28 | 26 | 0.154 | <0.693 |
| Financial-material circumstances | 6 | 4 | 1.339 | <0.247 |
| Parental neglect/inadequacy | 34 | 42 | 4.323 | <0.037 |
| Failure to thrive/medical health/handicap | 2 | 10 | 16.725 | <0.000 |
| Mother's mental health | 15 | 6 | 11.950 | <0.000 |
| Mother's physical health | 3 | 8 | 7.070 | <0.007 |
| Homelessness-housing | 10 | 4 | 7.953 | <0.004 |
| Suspected child abuse | 12 | 17 | 1.665 | <0.196 |
| Suspected child sexual abuse | 4 | 5 | 0.5930 | <0.441 |
| Delinquency | 6 | 9 | 1.053 | <0.304 |
| Non-school attendance | 3 | 9 | 10.521 | <0.001 |
| Child's behaviour | 9 | 13 | 2.615 | <0.105 |
| Other | 28 | 20 | 4.938 | <0.026 |
| (n) | 288 | 270 | | |

whilst there was a slight gender difference in general child abuse admissions, more girls were found to have been admitted for child sexual abuse (7 per cent compared to 2 per cent, $\chi^2$ 6.792, p<0.009). Also, although boys and girls were equally likely to be admitted into care where non-school attendance and child's behaviour were contributory factors, boys were significantly more likely to be admitted for reasons of delinquency than were girls (11 per cent boys compared to 3 per cent of girls, $\chi^2$ 12.225, p<0.000). Differential patterns in child sexual abuse and delinquency were also in existence at the initial stage of referral.

The proportion of children referred for certain reasons and subsequently admitted into care for those very reasons varied for black and white groups. For example, whilst similar proportions of black and white families were referred for reasons of poor housing and homelessness, significantly more black children were admitted into care where this was a contributory factor (10 per cent black compared to 4 per cent white, $p < 0.004$).

It was also found that while general trends remained the same as those at the referral stage, there were differences in the actual proportions of children being referred and admitted into care for particular reasons. This reflects a difference in perception between the referral agency and the Social Services Department. For example, where the reason was mother's mental health, greater proportions of black children were admitted into care than were actually initially referred. Similarly, the proportions of families in the category of parental neglect and inadequacy had risen quite markedly (22 per cent black, 33 per cent white at the stage of referral to 34 per cent black and 42 per cent white at the stage of admission).

## Length of time between referral and admission

An analysis of the length of time between the date of referral and the date of admission showed the speed with which children are admitted into care, and in particular revealed widespread disparities in the treatment of black and white children. Looking at the borough as a whole, it was found that 75 per cent of all children admitted into care were admitted within a year of referral. The majority were admitted within three months of referral (55 per cent).

The Pearson chi-square value in this case is 38.2 and the associated probability value is infinitesimally small. This extremely small probability denotes a high level of significance between the referral-admission time interval and the race and ethnicity of the child.

The computed infinitesimally low probability value can be attributed to those components (time intervals) which show significant black-white ratios. These components become obvious from a closer observation of the data. They include intervals in the range of 0–1 month, 7–12 months, 1–2 years and over 2 years (Fig. 3.3).

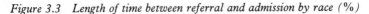

*Figure 3.3   Length of time between referral and admission by race (%)*

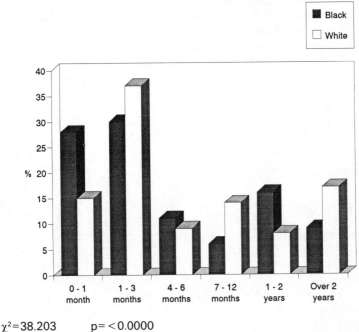

$\chi^2 = 38.203$         $p = < 0.0000$

We can see that black children are entering care much more quickly than white children. Of the black children who were in care, 28 per cent were admitted into care within four weeks of referral compared with only 15 per cent of white children (see Figure 3.3 above $p < 0.000$).

The mean number of months in care for the cohort was found to be 9.77. However, for black children (8.93), it was much lower than for white children (15.29). Black boys (8.56) came into care twice as quickly as white boys (16.87). There was a considerable difference between black girls (9.26) and white girls (13.17), however it was not as great as that between black boys and white boys.

Within the first four weeks following referral, more black girls were admitted into care than white girls (29 per cent black compared to 18 per cent white; ($\chi^2$ 16.669, $p < 0.005$).

Similarly, within the first four weeks following referral, more black boys were admitted into care than white boys (28 per cent black compared to 13 per cent white; ($\chi^2$ 25.916, p < 0.000).

In each of the four area offices, black children entered care more quickly than white children. In Areas 1 and 2, they came into care three times more quickly than white children.

## Legal status

A significant decision facing social workers at the stage of admission is to determine what particular legislation would be appropriate to use in the given circumstances. Two principal routes, voluntary and compulsory, existed at the time of this study in 1987 prior to the introduction of the 1989 Children Act. The voluntary route existed under Section 2 of the 1980 Child Care Act where an admission into care occurred following parental consent. Section 3 of this act made provisions for the local authority to assume rights and duties in the interests of the child. Assumptions of rights and duties meant that the local authority had statutory responsibility for the child, and the child was to all intents and purposes in compulsory care. Entry into care via the compulsory route happened in a number of different ways made possible by a variety of family and child care legislation (1969 CYPA, 1969 LRA, 1974 MCA).

For the purposes of this study, the legal status of children in care in Wenford Social Services Department was recorded at two stages, firstly, when the children entered care and secondly, at the time of the research.

### (a) Upon admission

Over half the cohort group (52 per cent) initially entered care via the voluntary route. Although there were no significant gender differences in these voluntary admissions, there were remarkable differences in terms of race. The proportion of black children entering voluntary care was much higher than that of white children (p < 0.000). This situation was found to exist throughout the borough in all four area offices. Black children were much less likely than white children to compulsorily enter care (p < 0.000, Fig. 3.4).

In the compulsory route, there were significant variations in the type of legislation chosen. Very few children entered care on a full care

*Figure 3.4    Legal status upon admission into care by race (%)*

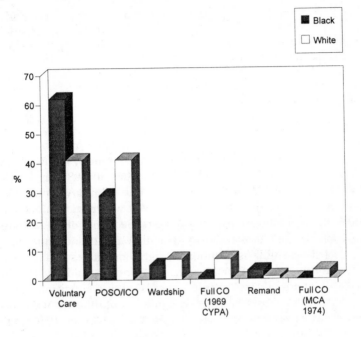

$\chi^2 = 50.454$          p= < 0.0000

order. The most common route of entry was the place of safety order (POSO) or the interim care order. All four area offices made considerable use of this route. These orders were usually made in cases of child abuse and neglect. There was little proportional difference in black and white girls admitted under these circumstances; black girls were as likely as white girls to be made subject to place of safety orders/interim care orders. However, overall compulsory powers were more frequently used in the case of white children. This applied to all routes of compulsory care except that of remand where black children (all boys) were more likely to be found. The most common route for a black child entering care was voluntary.

Wide variations were found between area offices in the use of wardship. Area 4 together with Area 3 had the lowest proportion of wardships while Areas 1 and 2 had the highest proportion of wardships.

## (b) At the time of the study

After a period of time in care, a great majority of the children in all four area offices had experienced a change in their legal status. Figure 3.5 in the Appendix depicts the borough wide situation. There were three main types of changes.

- from voluntary care to the assumption of parental rights and duties by the local authority.
- from a place of safety order/Interim care order (POSO/ICO) to a full care order.
- from voluntary care to wardship, or a full care order.

The study shows that black children were more likely to have parental rights assumed by the local authority than were white children. This was found to be the case in three of the four area offices. In Area 3, for example, 21 per cent of the black children had been made subject to 'assumptions of rights and duties' compared to only 11 per cent of white children.

In situations where children's legal status became compulsory, the gap which existed between black and white children at the admission stage was no longer so obvious. Black children were almost as likely as white children to be made subject to full care orders or wardships. In one area office (Area 2), they were much more likely to be made subject to a full care order under the 1969 Children and Young Persons Act (27 per cent black compared to 17 per cent white).

## Distribution of children in care by race

Figures 3.6a and 3.6b show the proportions of children by race in the care of Wenford Social Services Department, as well as the borough's child population. Only children between the ages of 0–15 were selected from the 'in care' population for this analysis. This is because child population figures could only be obtained for this group of children.

It can be seen in the figures below that in comparison with white children, there are lower proportions of black children in the general child population of the borough in each area office. In a comparison of 'in care' and 'in population', it is clear that black children are severely disproportionately over-represented in the care system, a situation that is reflected in all four area offices.

*Figure 3.6a   Black children in care (0–15 years) by area (%)*
*Black child population (0–15 years) by area (%)*

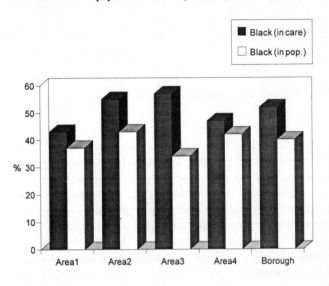

*Figure 3.6b   White children in care (0–15 years) by area (%)*
*White child population (0–15 years) by area (%)*

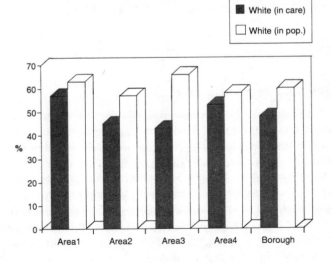

It should be noted that the situation of over-representation was not only in existence at the time of the study in 1987, but was found to have existed in previous years. Table 3.3 in the Appendix shows the proportions of children admitted into care from 1983 to 1986 and still found to be in care at the time of the study.

## Sex distribution of children in care

In terms of the actual proportions of children in care, there appeared to be significant findings in terms of gender. Table 3.4 shows sex distribution by ethnic origin. It can be seen that the proportion of white boys in care is significantly higher than white girls. For the ethnic groups in the black category, there appear to be some variations. African-Caribbean boys and girls appear to be equally likely to be in care. The proportion of girls from a Mixed-Origin background however is higher than boys, whereas the reverse is true for West African children. It needs to be emphasized that the actual numbers of White European, West African, Asian and Turkish Cypriot children are not significantly large to make any valid generalizations. However, the situation of African-Caribbean, Mixed-Origin and White Indigenous children is worthy of comparison. It is clear that white girls have a much lower chance of being admitted into care than black girls (African-Caribbean and Mixed-Origin).

## Age structure

### (a) Age upon entry into care

It was considered important to establish the age of children when they first entered care to determine the significance of age and admission into care. The findings of this study show that the majority of the cohort group were under the age of five when they entered care. About a third were between the ages of 6 to 12, and the remainder (just over a tenth) were between the ages of 13 to 16. The proportion of black children (58 per cent) who were under five upon entry into care was only slightly higher than that of white children (54 per cent). Also, the proportion of black adolescents (14 per cent) entering care was slightly higher than that of white adolescents (12 per cent). Thus,

*Table 3.4   Sex distribution by ethnic origin (%)*

| Ethnic Origin of child | Male | Female |
|---|---|---|
| White Indigenous | 57 | 43 |
| White European | 54 | 46 |
| African-Caribbean | 49 | 51 |
| Mixed-Origin | 47 | 55 |
| West African | 57 | 43 |
| Asian | 0 | 100 |
| Turkish Cypriot | 50 | 50 |
| Total | 52 | 48 |

$\chi^2 = 5.763 \; p < 0.016$

no significant differences were found between black and white children in terms of age upon entry into care (see Table 3.5 below).

## (b) Over-representation by age

In order to compare findings, the Wenford data were grouped into three age categories corresponding to the census data. It was found

*Table 3.5   Age upon entry into care by race (%)*

| Age group | Black | White | Borough |
|---|---|---|---|
| 0–5 years | 58 | 54 | 54 |
| 6–12 years | 28 | 34 | 32 |
| 13–16 years | 14 | 12 | 14 |
| Total % (n) | 100 (276) | 100 (259) | 100 (535) |

that the majority of the cohort (about two-thirds) fell into the middle category of 5–15 years. Slightly over a quarter of the cohort group were between the ages of 16–18, while the remainder fell into the youngest age category of 0–4.

A comparison by race of two of the three age groups 'in care' with the 'child population' further emphasized the over-representation of black children in the care of Wenford social services. An analysis of the borough's child population showed that black children comprised 38 per cent of the under-fives, while white children comprised 62 per cent of the under-fives. Thus although the proportion of black under-fives was lower in the general child population than white under-fives, it was higher in Wenford's 'in care' population; 55 per cent of the under-fives were black compared to 45 per cent who were white.

Similarly, in the case of 5–15 year olds, black children were again over-represented in the care system. The findings show that while black children comprised 41 per cent in the borough's child population, they comprised 51 per cent of the borough's 5–15 year olds in care.

It is more than likely that black children were over-represented in the 16–18 age group. It was not possible to compare these figures accurately with the census data because the age category did not correspond to those for which census data is available at this level of detail.

It seems that although there are no proportional differences between black and white groups in terms of age upon entry into care, a comparison of the findings with the census data reveals some interesting disparities.

## Discussion and analysis

Although previous research conducted into the situation of black children in the public care system has been patchy and limited, an attempt is made here to conceptualize the Wenford findings in the context of these studies.

One major factor which has been documented or accepted uncritically by various research studies is the disproportionate represen-tation of black children in care. The problematic nature of the terms 'disproportionate' and 'care' has received little attention. The high presence of black children in residential homes has often been understood to mean that black children are over-represented in care (NCH 1954, Rowe and Lambert 1973). The term 'care' has frequently been used in an ambiguous sense to imply care in general when in fact research studies have measured care only by virtue of a child being in a residential institution. Thus children placed in non-institutional settings, for example, foster families have not been included. So, when Rowe and Lambert (1973) asserted that black children spend longer periods in care, it has to be understood that care was used to mean residential care only. Also, the disproportionate representation of black children was not established by comparison with their actual numbers in the child population. Their high presence was taken as being indicative of over-representation.

Other research studies, although somewhat outdated, have demonstrated to various degrees and by various means the over-representation of black children in the care system (Gale 1963, Foren and Batta 1970, McCulloch, Batta and Smith 1974, Smith and Batta 1979, Lambeth 1980). The Lambeth study (1980), for example, found that in its random sample of 90 children in care, 54 per cent were black. This figure was then compared with the borough's black population of 18 per cent, and black children between the ages of 0–19 in the borough's population, and thus it was argued that black children were clearly disproportionately represented in the borough of Lambeth. What has to be recognized is that the Lambeth study was based upon a random sample of 90 children, 49 of whom were black. How representative this sample is of the borough or indeed other inner-city boroughs is questionable.

The Bradford studies conducted in the 1960s and 1970s asserted that there is a high rate of reception into care for Mixed-Origin children under the age of five (Foren and Batta 1970, McCulloch, Smith and Batta 1979, and Batta and Mawby 1981). This finding is not strictly comparable to the Wenford cohort group because of its focus on 'reception into care'. The Wenford research observed children in a 'snapshot' like fashion where all those found to be in care at one particular time were analysed rather than all those being admitted in a given period of time. By comparing 'in care' age groups to the child population figures the Wenford research was able to establish that black children of all age groups were over-represented in care, and that the majority of the cohort group were under the age of five when they entered care. The situation of Mixed-Origin children did not differ significantly from those of African-Caribbean origin who were the second largest group in the black category, after African-Caribbeans).

Recent research has asserted that children of Mixed-Origin are more likely to be admitted into care than those of African-Caribbean background or any other minority ethnic background (Bebbington and Miles 1989, Rowe et al 1989). Furthermore, it is said that children of Mixed-Origin are two-and-a-half times as likely to enter care as white children, and experience multiple admissions during their childhood. The Wenford study found no evidence to support these two studies either in the cohort or its sub-group inquiry which examined recent admissions into care.

The Wenford research in its study of the total 'in care' population has been able to document the over-representation of black children in care not only in terms of sheer numbers but in terms of other variables such as age and gender. Previous research has been able to shed little light on the age and gender of children entering care or in care. Research conducted on black children in care has failed to observe the differences and/or similarities in the situation of black boys and girls. Indeed, there has been a total denial of the existence of black girls in the care system, and most research has favoured a race rather than a race and gender perspective. A few research studies have focused on black boys in residential institutions pointing to the differential treatment received by these individuals (Lambert 1970, Pearce 1974, Cawson 1977, Pinder 1980). Overall however, in their documentation of the over-representation of black children, the various studies have failed to highlight the circumstances of black girls.

The Wenford research was designed to monitor the gender situation. In terms of over-representation, it was found that black girls were as likely as black boys to be found in care. The situation for white girls was different in that they were much less likely than white boys to be found in care. Black girls were, however, equally likely as white girls to be admitted into care for reasons of child abuse/child sexual abuse and be made subject to compulsory care. Both black and white girls were significantly less likely to be admitted into care for reasons of delinquency.

The circumstances under which black children enter care have received limited attention from other studies. Little is known of how black families come to be known to the social services and for what reason they become known. The high rate of referral by parents themselves (a third of all referrals) documented by the Wenford research, has been highlighted by other mainstream studies (Millham et al 1986, Fisher et al 1986). Also, there has been some evidence to suggest that significant proportions of black parents refer themselves to the social services (Boss and Homeshaw 1975). The Wenford study demonstrated that in terms of overall numbers the proportion of black parents referring themselves to the social services was in fact higher than that of white parents, but not significantly so. It appears therefore that black families are as likely as white families to seek the assistance of social services. It should be noted however that Asian families were severely under-represented.

Previous research suggests that black families are more likely than white families to be referred by other agencies such as the police, education and the health services (Boss and Homeshaw 1974, McCulloch, Smith and Batta 1979). The Wenford study found that although the proportion of black families referred by the police and the health service was higher, there was little significant proportional difference between black and white families. There was no significant evidence to support the findings of earlier studies which maintain that black families are more likely to be referred by agencies such as the police and the health and education service.

It is important to note however that the difference was observed not in the type of agency but in the reason for referral. That is, the reason for which black and white families were referred by any one particular agency was of significance. For example, it was found that more black mothers were referred by the police and the health service for reasons of mental health than were white mothers. Also, the proportion of black boys being referred by the police for reasons of delinquency was much greater than that of white boys.

Boss and Homeshaw (1975) found that 34 per cent of the black cases in their sample were referred by the families themselves, however, in terms of the actual reason for referral very few cases were referred for housing or financial difficulties. White families however were much more likely to refer themselves for these reasons. Boss and Homeshaw (1975) concluded that black families were less familiar with the fact that this kind of help was available from the social services. The Wenford study found no evidence to suggest that black families were less likely to refer themselves for socio-economic difficulties. In fact more black families referred themselves for housing difficulties than did white families.

The 'speed' at which children enter care after the date of referral has been explored in 'mainstream' studies (Millham et al 1986, Packman 1986). However, the situation of black children has been left unexamined. By using data drawn from social work case files, the Wenford research was able to ascertain that black children came into care much more quickly than white children. For example, in the first four weeks of referral, 28 per cent of the black children were admitted into care compared to only 15 per cent of the white children.

The first few weeks following referral are crucial since it is then that social work assessments are made. The questions which had to be asked were: why were black children admitted into care so quickly? What factors influenced social workers' decisions about black families? Were these different from white families? One may argue that these admissions were the result of voluntary agreements between parents and the Social Services Department since many of the black admissions were voluntary. However, the study shows that a great majority of the referrals were made by the police and the health service. Therefore the situation was not simply one where the parents were requesting care in each case. It has been suggested that social workers do not check the accuracy of the information presented to them by other agencies at the point of referral until the damage has been done, that is, once the child has been removed from his/her home environment (CARF 1983). Are social workers more willing to accept the problem definition imposed by other professionals (for example, doctors, health visitors, police officers) in the case of black families and children? If so, why? For the last few decades it has been argued that social workers lack an awareness and appreciation of the cultural complexities of black clients (Kent 1965, Triseliotis 1971, Cheetham 1972, Ahmed 1981, Arnold 1982, Liverpool 1986, Small 1984). Could it be that in the absence of this knowledge social workers feel under pressure to accept the perceptions of other professionals? Moreover, leaving cultural differences aside, what recognition is given to the effects of racial discrimination upon the lives of black service users?

Research into the perceptions of parents and social workers illustrates the differing understanding of the care process held by these individuals. In explanations of the initial entry into care, Pinder and Shaw (1974) found that while parents emphasized their socio-economic circumstances, social workers de-emphasized these and placed greater stress on family relationships. Unfortunately, Pinder and

Shaw (1974) presented their findings in a colour blind fashion because of the small number of black parents in their sample. Their study therefore puts forward a class perspective which overlooks the importance of race and ethnicity. Adams (1980) in his study of Lambeth Social Services found evidence to support Pinder and Shaw. However, he went further, asserting that black parents emphasized their socio-economic situation to a greater degree than white parents. Despite these assertions, both Pinder and Shaw (1974) and Adams (1980) presented a class perspective to the detriment of race and ethnicity. So while they acknowledged the disadvantaged position of black and white families, they made little attempt to explore the ways in which the issues of race and racism are handled in the social services.

Boss and Homeshaw (1974) argued that while the referral agencies appeared to be treating black families in a discriminatory fashion, they found no evidence to suggest that social workers operated along similar lines. The Wenford sub-group study found that social workers did hold negative attitudes towards black families which frequently influenced their decision making process.

Local authorities are under a duty to attempt to ameliorate the poor situation of families. The borough of Wenford has one of the largest budgets allocated to offer preventative help to families. Interviews with key social workers revealed that preventative work, where financial help (formerly under Section 1 of the 1980 Child Care Act, now Section 17 of the 1989 Children Act) and other assistance is offered to obviate the reception of children into care, was less likely to be done with black families and children. In the words of one black social worker:

> *Black Social Worker*: In my team I'm the only black social worker having to work with six other white social workers. My senior is white. In the whole area, all the seniors are white except one who's recently been appointed. So you have to work in a situation where there are predominantly white people, in a situation where white seniors are not looking at how white social workers are dealing with black clients but are monitoring how black social workers are working with white clients. That's a situation you are in. Also, when you get black clients on duty whereby you are suggesting financial assistance because that's all at the end of the day we're doing. We are not actually doing any preventative work here. We're just kind of giving out section 1 payments to the families. Then you hear a colleague of yours shouting across the room – 'repatriation', yeah, this kind of attitude is in the office you know.

Black social workers gave accounts of racial remarks made by their white colleagues consciously and unconsciously about black families. It was felt that this undoubtedly fed into their work with black families and children. It appeared that white social workers in one area office team often sent West African parents to the DSS knowing full well that they were not eligible for any social security benefits due to their student status in this country. This was apparently done to prove to themselves that these individuals were in need of financial help. If these families returned from the DSS (which was said to be rare after the initial rejection), this would be sufficient evidence of their desperate situation to make Section 1 monies available. Notions of deserving and non-deserving poor were very much in operation, and greatly heightened with the race dimension.

The pathological-pathogenic model, which assumes an ideology of assimilation and integration is important here (Denney 1983). According to this model, the responsibility for change should be placed on the individual client, however, due to the dynamics of the client-worker relationship, power is invested in the social worker to decide who is suitable for social work intervention. This means that 'certain racial groupings may be defined as unsuitable for intervention, and black clients, such as single mothers, may be deemed unsuitable for social work help' (Bryan 1992:176). The findings of the Wenford study show that low level and in some cases lack of preventive work with black families means that black children are admitted into care much more readily than white children.

In 1970, research was commissioned by the Home Office to explore the attitudes of social workers towards 'immigrant' clients (Kornreich et al 1973). About 12 per cent of the social workers with 'immigrant' clients (both black and white) held negative attitudes towards them. When colour could be isolated from 'immigrant' status, nearly 23 per cent of the workers showed a negative bias against black clients. For about a quarter of the social workers who had black clients who were all 'immigrants', the negative bias rose to 33 per cent.

Johnson (1986) asserts that racial stereotypes of black families are very much in existence in the 'caring professions', for example, 'Asian women keep to themselves', and 'West Indians believe in firm discipline administered in the home'. He points to the contradictions within these deeply held stereotypical views. That is, on the one hand such stereotypes are convenient when justifying the non-existence of appropriate service provision, however they conflict with the pathological notions of the black family 'that migrant families are incapable of fending for themselves, make poor adoptive parents and require more intervention than "normal families"' (Johnson 1986:85).

Stereotypes, whether positive or negative, are essentially caricatures. They simplify the complexities of people's lives, and serve a detrimental purpose. It is useful here to examine the adaptive-vitality model which points to the strengths of black families (Staples 1978, Karenga 1982). It has been argued that it is unhelpful to focus on the black family in a pathological manner, and that a recognition of the fact that the black family has survived the onslaught of slavery, colonialism, and imperialism is crucial (Small 1986). The black family is viewed as a distinct social grouping in its own right, and not as a negative deviation of the western nuclear family. Bryan argues that this type of perspective projects black women as 'strong and independent, forming alliances and fashioning a way of life as mothers which enables them to resist racism, and adapt "vitality" in the face of oppression' (Bryan 1992:176).

Bryan rightly points out that the adaptive-vitality model whilst challenging the negatives of the pathological school, has been subjected to criticism for creating its own negatives. It has to be recognized in the context of the personal social services that such models are not only misinterpreted in the face of a pool of ignorance, but also serve to justify a lack of intervention. For example, it may be convenient for a social services agency to hold on to the myth that black families have strong kinship bonds to abdicate its own responsibility. In the Wenford study, the low level of intervention with black families manifested itself in crisis situations resulting in the eventual admission of black children into care.

Information from interviews with white social workers illustrated the negative attitudes about black families which were used as rational explanations for their own decision making. In the case of a 15 year old African-Caribbean boy who was in voluntary care, the white social worker was in the process of sending this child to a community home outside the borough. This particular child had entered care after having stolen from his mother's purse. The mother had shown her disapproval by totally rejecting the child. In an interview, when the researcher asked whether the child had been in care previously, the social worker replied:

*White Social Worker*: No, he hasn't. His mother, she's got a very complicated history. I mean she's only 30 now. Richard is 15. She had

Richard when she was 14, her mother chucked her out. She was in care to another local authority. She's lived in several bed and breakfast places. But no, Richard hasn't been in care before.

By offering information which was not even asked, and furthermore by presenting a totally negative picture, the social worker demonstrated her pathological perspective of the black mother. This was further illustrated when the social worker made her perception more explicit. After a period of time in care, it was discovered that Richard had been truanting from school as well as engaging in solvent abuse. The social worker unhesitatingly attributed these problems as having stemmed from within the family:

> *White Social Worker*: Richard didn't seem to be locked into delinquent behaviour. It seemed that he had got into trouble because of his family problems, it wasn't the other way round. It looked as though the family problems were causing this. It looked as though he had been reacting against problems at home.

While some black children are no doubt in need of care and protection which the local authority attempts to provide, evidence suggests that social workers' negative attitudes about the black family clearly work to the detriment of other black children. The disproportionate representation of black children in care suggests that social workers fail to make effective assessments of black families' situation either through inability, ignorance and incompetence or due to the racist nature of policy, practice and provision. The pathological views of black families held by social workers undoubtedly informed their practice. When asked to offer explanations of why a child was admitted into care and was still found to be in care, social workers emphasized factors such as the mother's inability to cope as a single parent, absence of a father figure, as well as general conflict within the family home. Black parents, on the other hand, felt that the poor circumstances for which their children were taken into care had not improved at all. They felt powerless, helpless, and unable to change their situation. Some black parents felt totally dissatisfied with social services and stated that years of involvement had achieved very little for them and their children. Parents felt that they were almost invariably blamed for their situation:

> *Black Parent*: I would never go to them again. I'd rather struggle on my own. I've never had any satisfaction from the social workers; all the time they used to talk down to me. They used to blame me, I was the one who

was doing wrong and all that. They used to make me feel that I was a bad mother. They used to make me feel really guilty.

Another black mother whose ten year old son was admitted into care after sustaining an injury gave her perception of the circumstances:

*Black Parent*: It was my son Peter; he had hurt his finger. They (the social workers) said it was broken and that I broke it when I didn't. A week after this incident when Peter hurt himself, they had a meeting and came to my house with the police and took my son away.

The initial place of safety order under which the child was admitted into care later resulted in a wardship. The mother stated that she had been prevented from visiting her son in the children's home and was kept uninformed about social services plans of wardship:

*Black Parent*: I feel very bitter that my son has been made a ward of court without my knowledge. I've been told this can last until he's 18. I am going to court on the 26th of this month; the court wants to see if there's been any changes in my circumstances. They don't want me to work; but I can't stay at home.

The above case illustrates the feelings of helplessness of a black mother regarding her child's compulsory legal status. It should be stressed that while the majority of black children entered care via the voluntary route, a significant proportion entered care on a place of safety order or an interim care order. The majority of these children were made subject to compulsory care after a period of time in care. Also, higher proportions of black children than white children had their voluntary care status changed to compulsory care. The implications of this change in legal status are discussed in the following two chapters.

While parents expressed their feelings of disengagement from the decision making process, the children in the sub-group felt the least involved in the whole situation. The children felt confused about what had happened or was going to happen to them. When asked what led up to her reception into care, one African-Caribbean girl stated:

*Black Child*: I couldn't really say. It's all a bit confusing, a bit hard for me to even understand. The way I see it is that me and my mom just couldn't get on under the same roof.

The children often imbibed the views of social workers or foster carers, and tended to blame their parents for the situation. John, a West African child was admitted into care following a police referral. The police found bruises on John's arm which led them to take out a place of safety order. John, in explaining his admission into care could only see where his mother was at fault:

> *Black Child*: It was because my mom kept on beating me, when I came home after school. I was on the bus, the bus conductor took me to the police.

After much prompting, John conceded that he was responsible for some of what happened between him and his mother, for example, he consistently went home late from school. Ahmed (1981) argues that social workers often take the side of the child and fail to gain the parent's perception of the situation. It is argued that social workers jump on the culture bandwagon and fail to explore other possibilities. John's social worker was a typical example of this, she had less to say about the actual injuries but talked incessantly about the West African culture. Apart from maintaining that West African parents are disciplinarian and dictatorial, she very emphatically stated that John's early childhood separation from his mother was the cause of the problem:

> *White Social Worker*: He had a very marked foreign accent. In the conversation, it came out that he'd been born here, but sent back to live with his granny in Sierra Leone when he was only two. He had then come back 18 months ago. So he was feeling very strange. It was like a culture shock to him.

The above quote illustrates that while social workers attempt to empathize with children, often inappropriately, they very rarely empathize with the parent's situation. It was in these situations that children often felt that care was a much better alternative to their own home environment. They liked the freedom which was permitted.

## Summary and conclusion

It is clear that there are differences in the referral and admission patterns of black and white children. The Wenford study has demonstrated, in quantitative terms, the disproportionate representation of black children in the care system. It has also been able to explore the importance of age and gender variables, as well as the wider issues of entry into care; areas which had hitherto received little attention.

While a recognition is made of the disadvantaged position of black families in the areas of housing and employment, and therefore the greater likelihood of such families to need social services help, this study has concerned itself with documenting the ways in which social workers process such cases. It is shown that while there are no significant proportional differences in the referrals made by agencies such as the police and the health service, there are differences in the reasons for which these same agencies referred black and white families. Moreover, the evidence suggests that social workers approached cases of black children and families with a greater degree of negativity than those of white children and families. Such negative attitudes operated to the detriment of black children and families.

# 4

# *Placement in Care*

Although the placement of black children in white substitute homes has been the focus of study for the last few decades, there has been no comprehensive account of the paths and destinations of black children in the care system. This chapter offers an account of the process of placement for black children in care. In an examination of the quantitative and qualitative findings, various factors which influence social worker decision-making, for example, legal status of child, age, race and ethnicity, and social services policy are discussed in detail. The type of placement in which a child was likely to be found was recorded at three intervals. Firstly, when the child was admitted into care, secondly at the time of the early part of the research in 1987, and finally six months after the initial research was conducted. The findings below are presented for these three stages. The chapter also addresses the policy and practice of 'same race' and 'transracial' placements in the borough of Wenford.

## *Placement upon admission*

Research evidence suggests that admissions into care are invariably a result of a crisis situation (Millham et al 1986, Packman 1986). In the previous chapter it was shown that 55 per cent of the cohort were admitted into care within three months of referral. Such admissions inevitably determine the type of setting in which a child may initially be placed. For example, children admitted into care for reasons of failure to thrive and child abuse are usually placed in hospital settings while medical examinations are carried out. These placements are generally short-term, and other arrangements have to be made after the initial crisis period. The children's circumstances are reassessed after the admission phase and decisions are then reached about their short-term and long-term care.

Figure 4.1 below shows the type and range of placements in which

*Figure 4.1   Placement upon admission by race (%)*

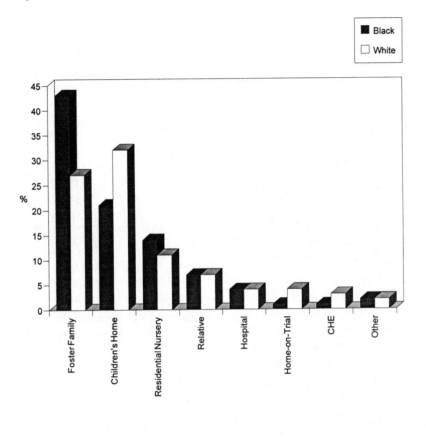

$\chi^2 = 25.370$        p= < 0.001

children in the cohort group found themselves upon admission into care.

It can be seen that children were most likely to be found in three types of settings (foster family, children's home, and residential nursery). If a distinction is drawn between family and institutional placements, black children are represented in similar proportions in both of these settings. White children, however, are concentrated in institutional settings. Only 38 per cent of the white children were placed in family settings compared to 51 per cent of black.

61

## (a) Foster family

Although more black children than white children were placed in substitute families, there was little proportional difference between black and white under-fives in terms of their prospects of being placed in foster family settings. However, there were differences between the other two age groups. While greater numbers of white 6–12 year olds were placed in substitute families (39 per cent compared to 29 per cent), greater numbers of black adolescents (13–18 years) were found in such placements (36 per cent compared to 24 per cent). The overall differences between black and white children were also reflected in a comparison of black and white girls.

There were significantly more black girls than white girls placed in foster families; almost half of the black girls (47 per cent) in the cohort group found themselves in foster families compared to only 27 per cent of the white girls. A comparison of boys showed that while there were more black boys than white boys placed in foster families, the difference was not significant.

## (b) Children's home

It was interesting to observe that while black children were significantly represented in substitute families, white children tended to be placed in children's homes. Very few black girls were found in this type of setting; only 15 per cent of them were placed in children's homes compared to 34 per cent of the white girls.

On the whole, the borough's own children's homes were used to place these children, that is, the children were not placed in homes outside the borough. The distance of placement often jeopardizes parental links and the implications of this are discussed in the next chapter. Of the black children who were placed in children's homes, the majority were adolescents, 78 per cent were between the ages of 13–18, while only 22 per cent were between the ages of 6–12. Amongst those found in children's homes, there were no significant differences in terms of age between black and white groups.

## (c) Observation and assessment centre (O&A), and Children's homes with education on the premises (CHEs)

These residential institutions are different from ordinary children's homes in that they admit children who cannot normally be assessed or contained in ordinary children's homes. Observation and Assessment centres are short-stay assessment settings and children move on very quickly into other placements. Children's homes with education on the premises (CHEs, formerly known as Approved Schools) are institutions where more 'unruly' children who cannot be contained in ordinary children's homes or who are persistently truanting from school are generally placed. Both types of institutions impose stricter discipline than ordinary children's homes.

Previous research has shown that high numbers of black children are to be found in such settings, particularly CHEs, often for reasons of parental conflict (Lambert 1970, Pearce 1974, Cawson 1977, Pinder 1982). This research study shows that in the borough of Wenford, very few children (both black and white) were placed in such institutions. In terms of race there was no overall pattern in existence which could be applied to the whole borough. For example, while in Area 1, more black children than white were placed in Observation and Assessment centres, this was not the case in Area 2 and Area 3 where more white children than black were placed in such institutions.

There were no proportional differences between black and white boys, about a tenth of each group was placed in these settings. However, more white girls than black girls were found in these institutions, 11 per cent of the white girls were placed here compared to only 6 per cent of the black girls. This is possibly because fewer black girls than white entered care for reasons of delinquency, non-school attendance and behavioural problems (see Chapter Three).

## (d) Residential nursery

Children under the age of seven are sometimes placed in residential nurseries. Quite a sizeable proportion of the cohort was initially placed in this type of setting. Differential patterns were observed between black and white groups; for example, while in Area 1 and Area 4, there were more white children placed in residential nurseries, in Area 2 and Area 3 there were more black children placed in such settings. However, looking at the borough as a whole, it was found that while there was not a significant difference, a slightly greater number of black children (14 per cent) than white children (11 per cent) were placed in residential nurseries. Of the black children placed in residential nurseries, the majority were girls.

### (e) Hospitals

Children admitted into care for reasons of failure to thrive and child abuse are often placed in hospital settings. In the previous chapter, it was shown that quite a significant proportion of children were admitted into care following allegations of child abuse.

Although in Area 1, significantly more black children were placed in hospital settings, there was no overall proportional difference. Also, no differences were found in terms of gender.

### (f) Relatives

Children are sometimes placed with relatives where the local authority provides financial assistance. The borough of Wenford made payments available to relatives on a par with foster carers. In Area 2 and Area 3, more white children than black were placed with relatives while more black children than white were placed with relatives in Area 1 and Area 4. While there were proportional differences between black and white groups within areas, there was no overall difference. The majority of the children placed with relatives were older children. There were no proportional differences between boys and girls placed with relatives.

### (g) Home on Trial (HOT)

On occasions, children are technically admitted into care but remain placed with their parents. These types of placements often occur when the local authority lacks an appropriate placement and/or it is not considered a risk to leave the child in the family home. Children who are placed Home on Trial from the beginning are often those on care orders for reasons of delinquency and/or non-school attendance. The Wenford research showed that more white children than black were placed with their natural parents, 5 per cent of white boys compared to 2 per cent of black boys, and 3 per cent of white girls compared to no black girls.

The majority of the children placed Home on Trial were from the older age group (13–18). All the children were on compulsory care orders.

### (h) Other

Some children were placed in settings other than those named in the questionnaire. The numbers were much too small to make valid generalizations. However, it needs to be noted that there were children placed in settings such as bed and breakfast hotels, and hostels run by registered charities, for example, Barnardos. These were normally older children who were due to leave care on reaching the age of 18 or 19, and for whom other placements were not considered appropriate.

## Placement at the time of study

It was decided to record the type of placement in which a child was found at the time of the research to measure the differences between placements upon admissions and placements after a period of time in care. The results are presented in Figure 4.2 in the Appendix. It should be noted that there were possibilities of some children having had several different placements in the period between admission and the time of the research study. Information related to this is presented later in the chapter.

With the exception of Area 1, black children were still more likely to be placed with foster families than to be concentrated in children's homes or other institutional settings. No significant differences were found in age between black and white groups placed with families.

The proportion of white children in children's homes, and CHEs was still higher than black children. This pattern was in existence in all four areas.

The greater likelihood of white children being placed Home on Trial was again confirmed. It was found that white children in all four areas were more likely to be placed with their natural families than were black children.

At the time of the research, there was a five-fold increase in the number of children placed Home on Trial. A majority of these were again white. Most of the children were from the older age group. White under-fives were more likely to be placed Home on Trial than black under-fives, however there were no significant differences in the other two age categories.

The situation of placements with relatives was not dissimilar from that of the initial inquiry. More black children than white were placed with relatives in Area 1 and Area 3, while more white children than black were placed with relatives in Area 2. There was little overall difference.

65

Quite a sizeable number of children were now concentrated in 'other' placements. There were great area variations and there was no consistent pattern in terms of race.

The gender patterns which existed at the initial stage of admission were very much in existence at the time of the research.

## Placement upon follow-up

Six months after the initial information was recorded, a follow-up study of the same children showed that the pattern of placements which existed at the initial stage of admission, and at the initial stage of the study had not changed greatly. The findings are presented for the borough as a whole in Figure 4.3 in the Appendix.

The rates of difference between black and white groups can be seen very clearly. More black children than white are represented in foster family settings, more white children than black are concentrated in institutional settings like children's homes, and CHEs. A greater number of white children than black children are placed home on trial. There is virtually no difference in the proportion of black and white children who are placed with relatives. One difference from the earlier findings is that more black children than white are found in 'other' placements.

## Total number of placements

It was shown in the last chapter that many of the children in the cohort (over 50 per cent) had been in care previously, some more than once. Although the Wenford research focused on the current care episode, it was considered important to record how many placements children had actually experienced in all their care episodes. Table 4.1 in the Appendix depicts the findings which relate to all and not solely the current care episode.

It can be seen that there are virtually no differences in the proportions of black and white children in terms of total number of placements. They are equally likely to have had several placements. Not surprisingly, a majority of the children who had had the greatest number of placements were adolescent children who had been in care more than three times previously.

A correlation was found between length of stay in care and number of placements. It was found that a quarter of the cohort group had been in care for more than ten years. These children had had the greatest number of placements. There was little significant difference between black and white groups.

## Transracial placements

In theoretical terms, a transracial placement is one where a child is placed in a substitute family which is racially and/or culturally different from their own. However, in the context of British society, a transracial placement is one where a black child is placed in a white family, and not vice versa. The practice of transracial placements began in the 1950s and still exists today. The factors leading up to this and the implications of such practice as outlined by researchers and practitioners are discussed elsewhere (Gill and Jackson 1983, Weiss 1988, Rhodes 1992).

The borough of Wenford had adopted a policy which stipulated that children should be placed in families which were racially and culturally similar to their own. This policy was to be applied to new admissions into care, and not to children who were already in care in transracial placements. It was felt that children who were placed transracially were settled in their families and it would not be in their interests to be moved.

### (a) Upon admission

It was not surprising to find that while there were black children placed in white foster family settings, no white children were placed in transracial family settings. In a comparison of African-Caribbean, Mixed-Origin and West African children, it was found that African-Caribbean children were less likely to be placed transracially. This is indicative of the availability of foster carers from the African-Caribbean community. The availability of African-Caribbean foster carers was such that minority ethnic children from Asian and Turkish

*Table 4.2  Ethnic origin of foster family by ethnic origin of child (%)*

**EO of FF**                                      **Ethnic Origin of Child**

|            | WI | WE | AC | MO | WA | A | TC | Total |
|------------|-----|------|-----|-----|------|------|------|-------|
| **White I**  | 100 | 75  | 13 | 43 | 33 | 0   | 100 | 58 |
| **White E**  | 0   | 25  | 1  | 3  | 0  | 0   | 0   | 1.5 |
| **African-C**| 0   | 0   | 86 | 46 | 50 | 100 | 0   | 38 |
| **Mixed**    | 0   | 0   | 0  | 8  | 0  | 0   | 0   | 2 |
| **West A**   | 0   | 0   | 0  | 0  | 17 | 0   | 0   | .5 |
| Total (%) (n) | 41 (109) | 1.5 (4) | 28 (76) | 23 (61) | 4 (12) | 1 (3) | 1.5 (4) | 100 (269) |

$\chi^2 = 238.728$ p = $< 0.000$
Key:
WI—White Indigenous; WE—White European; AC—African-Caribbean;
MO—Mixed-Origin; WA—West African; A—Asian; TC—Turkish Cypriot;
FF—Foster Family

Cypriot background were also placed in these settings (see Table 4.2 above). The policy and practice concerns of such a situation are discussed later in this chapter.

### (b) Upon follow-up

The proportion of children placed with foster families fell from 269 to 244 at the follow-up stage, however the proportion of black children placed transracially remained the same.

## Discussion and analysis

In the quantitative inquiry, the Wenford research focused generally on the type of placement in which a child was found. Interviews with social workers, parents and children provided an insight into the process of placement. The quantitative findings are therefore analysed in the context of the perceptions of principal individuals.

## Family vs residential placements

Although much has been written on the placement of black children, the focus of such writings has been limited in scope (Rowe and Lambert 1973, Raynor 1969, Jackson 1975, Gill and Jackson 1983, Lambert 1970, Pearce 1974, Cawson 1977). The practice of transracial placements and the representation of black children in children's homes have transcended all other aspects of the placement process. For example, the issues of age, gender, the number of placements and social services policy, practice and provision have not been addressed.

Previous research has documented that black children are more likely to be over-represented in institutional settings (NCH 1954, Gale 1963, Rowe and Lambert 1973, Lambert 1970, Pearce 1974, Cawson 1977, Dale 1986). In a study of long-term children in care, Rowe and Lambert (1973) found that 552 of the children in their sample were black, that is, one child in every five. They state that 388 of these children were confined to residential institutions and that only 164 were deemed to be suitable for substitute family placements. Such studies have asserted that due to the difficulty of finding suitable family placements for black children, they have tended to be concentrated in residential institutions. More recently, Dale (1986) has argued that black children languish in residential institutions as a consequence of social services' 'same race' policies. Other studies have stated that due to the 'behaviourial difficulties', differential police activity, and delinquency, black children have been disproportionately represented in CHEs (Lambert 1970, Pearce 1975, Cawson 1977). The overwhelming finding has been that black children are over-represented in residential establishments.

The Wenford findings showed that the reverse situation was in existence. That is, more white children than black were placed in institutional settings. It was found that black children had a much better chance of being placed in substitute family settings than white children. This pattern of placement was in existence at the time of the initial admission as well as at subsequent intervals of the research.

There is clearly a conflict between the Wenford research findings, and the findings of previous research. There are a number of factors which have to be explored to understand this conflict. Firstly, much of the previous research is now outdated. It could be argued that the situation has changed and that the results of the earlier studies no longer hold true. Secondly, the geographical scope of the studies

69

means that they are not strictly comparable. For example, Rowe and Lambert (1973) studied 28 different agencies, while the Wenford research is a study of one local authority Social Services Department. Thirdly, while the Wenford research focused on the total number of children who were admitted into care and their various placements destinations, other studies have limited their focus to residential institutions. This has meant that they have not been able to draw comparisons between those placed in alternative settings. It is important to note that most of the Observation and Assessment centres and CHEs used by the borough of Wenford were private resources outside London. These institutions were also used by other local authorities. Thus there were probably black children there from other areas. The Wenford study observed only the placement patterns of children in the care of Wenford, and was not designed to establish the black/white ratio of residential institutions. A study of these institutions may have shown that there were higher numbers of black children than white in these settings. The Wenford research cannot confirm or refute previous findings because of the differing foci and methodologies employed in the research design of various studies.

In the last few decades, child care practice emphasis has shifted towards family placements which are much preferred to residential institutions (Rowe and Lambert 1973, Thoburn 1987). The permanency principle has meant a move away from institutional care to foster care, and is intertwined into 'good social work practice'. More importantly, the need to find appropriate families which are racially and culturally suitable is now enshrined into the child care legislation (Sec.22 (5) (c), Children Act 1989).

In the borough of Wenford, the child care policy regarding the placement of children in substitute families stipulated that children should be placed in families which were racially and culturally similar to their own. This was well established practice in the borough of Wenford long before the introduction of the 1989 Children Act. Thus, it is to Wenford's credit that the same race policy did not remain a mere paper policy. The borough made a commitment to support the policy by providing sufficient resources to make it a reality to place children in racially and culturally appropriate foster care settings. In 1987, a journalist stated that 67 per cent of the foster carers in the borough of Wenford were black. While the accuracy of this assertion is questionable since the department itself does not claim to know the situation, it is clear that there is a sufficient pool of substitute black families available. This explains the greater likelihood of black children to be placed in family settings.

Why were white children more likely to be concentrated in institutional settings? We know from the previous chapter that white children were more likely to be admitted into care for reasons of 'delinquency', 'non-school attendance', and 'child's behaviour'. Their legal status was more likely to be compulsory. Recent evidence suggests that adolescents admitted into care compulsorily are more likely to be placed in residential institutions (Fisher et al 1986). In their study of Sheffield Social Services Department, Fisher et al (1986) found that two-thirds of the compulsorily admitted children were placed in reception facilities (including O & A centres and CHEs), one quarter were placed in family group homes and only 6 per cent were fostered. Since the majority of black children enter care via the voluntary route they are more likely to be placed in foster family settings. Voluntary admissions are normally intended to be short-term, and the likelihood of children to be placed in foster families is greater since the availability of short-term foster carers is greater. Factors such as reason for admission, compulsory care status, and age of white children indicate that their chances of being placed in institutional settings were greater.

There has been no research into placement breakdown and race and ethnicity. The Wenford research findings show that placement breakdown patterns were similar for white and black groups. More research is needed in this area at a qualitative level to explore factors leading to breakdown.

## Same race placement policy

The Wenford study provides the first evaluative account of same race placement policy. The findings point to the conflicts and constraints in matching substitute parents and children. Notions of race, ethnicity, culture, religion and language as enshrined in the 1989 Children Act are important considerations in the placement of children. In the borough of Wenford, the broad availability of African-Caribbean and the virtual non-existence of other minority ethnic foster carers often resulted in a mismatch of placements. Social workers expressed concern about the placement, in African-Caribbean families, of Mixed-Origin, West African, Asian and Turkish Cypriot children.

71

## (a) Children of Mixed-Origin

Factors explaining the higher incidence of black children's placement in foster families have been highlighted above. One of the major determinants responsible for the placement of black children in substitute families and particularly black foster families was said to be the adoption of the 'same race placement' policy. There was a ready pool of black families available in which black children could be placed. However, the policy was not without problems. While social workers felt clear about the placement of African-Caribbean children in African-Caribbean families, they were less clear about the situation of Mixed-Origin children. The previous chapter showed that 36 per cent of the black children in care were children of Mixed-Origin. They were the second largest group of black children in care after African-Caribbeans.

According to the 1984-1986 Labour Force Surveys, 27 per cent of married and cohabiting African-Caribbean men aged 30 and 28 per cent of married and cohabiting women of the same age had white partners (Central Statistics Office 1988). It has been asserted that children of these unions are greatly over-represented in care (Rowe et al 1989, Bebbington and Miles 1989). Our research shows however, that the vast majority of Mixed-Origin children in the care of Wenford Social Services Department had a white mother and a black African-Caribbean father. There were very few children who had a white father and a black African-Caribbean mother. This suggests that Mixed-Origin children from one particular type of union are more likely to be in care than others. Research is needed in this area to explore why such children are over represented in the care system.

In the borough of Wenford, the children of Mixed-Origin presented difficulties for the social workers. On the whole, black social workers perceived Mixed-Origin children as black and regarded a black family or a Mixed-Origin family as a suitable placement. Most white social workers and some black social workers found themselves caught in a dilemma when dealing with Mixed-Origin children. Their arguments ranged from 'client self-determination' to 'culture shock' and 'identity' issues. There were those social workers who argued that the wishes of the child and the mother (who in many cases was white) should be respected, and saw the departmental policy as 'very aggressive and watertight' which denied the principle of client self-determination. The following extract from an interview with a social worker illustrates this argument.

*Social Worker*: The child care policy is that you've got to culturally match children but this cultural matching doesn't take into account mixed-race children, and doesn't take into account mothers' views. It seems that every time there is a mixed-race child in care, we tend to take the father's side who may be a black person, and want to give the kid a black identity. But I think its equally important to consider the mother's view on this and work towards coming to a conclusion whether the child needs to be identified as black or not.

I think the social worker involved should make an effort to bring together the views of the two parents. I think the policy of transracial placements should be flexible. It should depend on the individual, since the whole of social work is based on individual need. I think the policy is imposing. I'm not in a game of imposing. I'm in a game of partnership with my clients. I'm there to advise them.

The above quotation typifies the general feeling of many social workers working with Mixed-Origin children. When the above social worker was asked how the Mixed-Origin children with whom he had worked perceived themselves, he replied that '99 per cent of them see themselves as black'. When asked whether these children would want to be placed in white families, he stated that he had not come across any Mixed-Origin child who did. The question which has to be asked is 'who is the client'? In whose interests do we carry out policies? Are we exercising our own ideological notions; or are we attempting to provide the best possible care for the client?

Social workers' pathological perceptions of black families were very much in existence. While they accepted the placement of African-Caribbean children in African-Caribbean families, they felt that a white family would be better for other Mixed-Origin children:

*Social Worker*: I had a child who was half Irish and half Singhalese, and they (*fostering and adoption*) wanted me to place him with either a Caribbean or an African family. And I said 'no'. It's ridiculous, I'd rather place him in a white family.

Cheetham (1981) further highlights this point by illustrating the reluctance of white social workers to place white children in black families. She found that even when a placement was a short-term one, and there were black families available while white families were not, social workers were reluctant to place children in these families. Similarly, in the case of Mixed-Origin children, social workers in the borough of Wenford engaged in discourse on the shades of colour

73

when deciding upon a family placement for these children. Comments such as 'this is almost a white child in a black family' were not uncommon. There were numerous misguided notions of identity on the part of the social workers. A Mixed-Origin child was invariably seen to be the property of the white mother who after all it was argued had been looking after him in the absence of the father, and deserved to have her wishes taken into account. In the context of broken relationships within mixed-partnerships, Brummer (1988) signals the dangers of white workers colluding with the white parent. She asserts that 'children of mixed-parentage need both a sense of belonging and the capacity to negotiate differences. The principle which should underpin good practice is that identity issues require exploration rather than denial' (Brummer 1988:83).

The notion that Mixed-Origin children are essentially black is understood to a greater degree by the children themselves and their parents (both black and white). However, this black identity does not exist from the start but emerges in later adolescent years. White mothers of Mixed-Origin children emphasized the traumas their children had experienced in the formulation of this identity. Mothers themselves acknowledged that they had not always played a positive role in this process. When asked whether her adolescent son saw himself as black, one mother replied:

> *Mother*: I wouldn't know because that never arises in this family. The colour doesn't enter into it. I mean I wouldn't have gone with their father if I didn't want half-caste children.

The same mother stated that when her son was five years old, she found him daubing himself white with white emulsion paint. This had apparently happened because children at school had teased the boy about his colour. The mother's only response (rather insensitively) was that 'it was a good job it was emulsion and not gloss'.

White natural mothers of Mixed-Origin children, while unable to see their children as black, made no objections to their placement in African-Caribbean families. Most white mothers in fact praised the level of care being offered by black foster carers:

> *Mother A*: . . . he knows both anyway, that doesn't bother me. I mean there's good and bad isn't there? There's good and bad in every race. She's a very nice lady.

> *Mother B*: They're doing all right. The foster mother is very good. She fights with the social worker to get things for them. She is also fighting

with the social worker regarding sending the children home for Christmas. The children want to come home, and the foster mother has expressed their view to the social worker.

Although individual social workers expressed their feelings in research interviews about the situation of Mixed-Origin children, there was no collective opposition to the placement of Mixed-Origin children in African-Caribbean families. The centralized power structure meant that social workers had little or no say in the formulation of policies. They found themselves being dictated to by policies which they could do little but implement according to the wishes of higher management. The major policies which social workers resented were the 'same race placement' policy, the 'private and voluntary placement' policy (where social workers had to present their case before a panel before funding could be approved for such placements) and 'closure of children's homes' policy. Social workers felt undermined and deskilled, and perceived such policies as an attack upon their professionalism:

> *Social Worker*: For example, Wenford have got the same-race placement policy which I agree with. But I would say that, it should not be said that it must be, it should be left to professionals who have got a professional knowledge base and who should decide what's best for the child. You can't have a blanket policy like that.

As already mentioned, although social workers made comments such as the one above, there was no collective voice to argue that social workers as professionals could decide what was in the client's best interests. Where social workers did organize in opposing higher management was in the area of industrial relations where their pay and lack of resources in terms of staff recruitment were the issues. One area office was regularly closed to the public two or three days a week while negotiations were continuing with higher management. In this situation, neither higher management nor the professional social workers expressed the client's best interests.

## (b) 'Marginalized' black children

The Wenford cohort study showed that while African-Caribbean and Mixed-Origin children were the two largest groups of black children in care, there was a small proportion of West African, Asian and Turkish Cypriot children also in care. The placement of these

75

children in substitute families presented difficulties in relation to the departmental policy of 'same race placements'. The only families which were available for the placement of these children were African-Caribbean families, and the only individuals who felt strongly about the placement of these children in African-Caribbean families were social workers who were of similar origin as the children. This created a great deal of bad feeling amongst the staff:

> Social Worker A: I understand that there are a lot of Afro-Caribbean children in care, but they've actually kind of prioritized that to the extent of marginalizing the other groups which I think is really bad.

> Social Worker B: What I'm worried about in Wenford is that they seem to be doing quite a lot for the Afro-Caribbeans, a lot of good work there, what I'm worried about is the Asian kids. I think little effort has been made.

> Social Worker C: The policy fails when it comes to Asian children. There are no foster families from the Asian communities. It seems that no efforts have been made to recruit Asian foster families.

While West African, Asian and Turkish Cypriot social workers felt very strongly that children should be placed in families which were racially and culturally similar to their own, white social workers had little awareness of children's cultural background giving them little ground on which to argue where these children should be placed. On the whole, the latter tended to work within the defined framework. The following white social worker had two Asian children placed in a short-term African-Caribbean family, when asked whether a long-term Asian family would be sought in the future, she replied:

> Social Worker: Ideally, I suppose, its difficult to know. I don't think we are particularly well off in terms of Asian foster parents. It depends which way you look at it. They (the children) are not particularly familiar with the Asian culture.

When asked what religion the children were, the social worker replied after a long pause by saying, 'I don't think I've ever known that'. This particular social worker was not alone in her ideas of working within the boundaries drawn out by her superiors. A social worker's role as a mere bureaucrat is clearly summed up here, and conflicts with the view presented earlier in this chapter where social workers resented the imposition of policies and wished to assert their professionalism.

## *Transracial placements*

Although black children were no longer placed in white substitute families, the plight of those black children placed in transracial settings prior to the introduction of the 'same race placement' policy has to be recognized. The significant proportion of black children found to be in white families had remained there because it was considered not to be in the child's interests to move them after a considerable length of time in these settings. The negative experiences of these children were noted from the case files. A few case study examples are given below to illustrate the experiences of such children.

One of the most disturbing cases was of a West African boy who had experienced a series of white foster placement breakdowns. He was now 18, and diagnosed as schizophrenic. His file stated that he 'finds it difficult to accept his racial/cultural origin'. The West African children were often given English names as substitutes to their African names, and the implications of this for the identity of these children were enormous.

In another case, of a 12 year old African-Caribbean boy, the review report read:

> The child has accepted their values and identifies completely with them. He has no illusions of having turned, overnight, into a white man and jokes with them about the name 'chalky', and they laugh with him and call him a 'coon'.

Recent case file notes revealed that this child's behaviour became 'aggressive' towards foster carers. This resulted in the breakdown of that foster placement.

One African-Caribbean girl was placed with white foster parents in Hampshire. Several problems had been mentioned, and the child's relationship with the foster carers was said to be poor. In a letter to her social worker in 1985, the child wrote:

> This sort of life was alright for me when I was younger because I deserved it. I think that one of the happiest times of my life was when I was at the Children's Home. I would love to go back there, because I felt there were more of my kind there. Please don't force me to stay here because I'm only fostered not adopted.

The above cases offer a glimpse of the plight of transracially placed black children. There is no comprehensive study to date which has explored their pain and anguish in an adequate manner. It would appear inevitable that the majority of these young children fostered or adopted by white couples, before the 'same race placement' policy came into being, will suffer the consequences in later years.

## Perceptions of care

Interviews with parents and children demonstrated their concerns and needs. Participants were encouraged to talk freely about their experiences of family and institutional settings. Black parents' views about black foster carers ranged from 'stricter discipline' to racial and cultural considerations. Natural parents wanted black foster families who would enforce good discipline and exert control over the children. The role of the black foster carer was perceived by parents to be a continuation of their own role. Such placements were invariably seen in a highly positive light. Parents felt able to relate to black foster mothers and found them very accessible. Consequently, as we shall see in the next chapter, this enabled them to maintain better contact with their children.

Jenkins (1981) in the North American context found that black parents' primary concern was for a 'loving home'. The Wenford study does not support this. Parents were very aware of the negative implications of transracial placements and wanted their children to be placed in black families. Only a tiny minority of parents expressed their views in a colour blind fashion, that is, they did not prefer one ethnic group of foster carers to the other. It is instructive to note that in Jenkins' research, the choice of a 'loving home' or 'similar ethnic group' was presented as if these terms are mutually exclusive. This quite possibly affected the parents' response.

Black children were able to talk about the benefits of foster placements not only in terms of their physiological but also emotional needs. They expressed feelings of being safe, secure and comfortable in foster families racially and culturally similar to themselves. Their relief at 'being able to be themselves' was voiced with great jubilation. Black foster carers were presented as having a good understanding of dietary, hair and skin care needs. Both parents and children felt that because of their position in this society, black foster carers were able to appreciate the impact of racism upon the lives of black families. It was stated that such understanding was a prerequisite for parents and foster carers to work in partnership.

Children, however, while recognizing the need for a black family felt at pains to point out what they saw as the bad features of their placements. These views were expressed by children who had had previous care episodes and had experienced more than one foster placement. In some instances, placement breakdown and the label of 'difficult' had become a central feature of their care career:

> *Child*: She used to try and beat me up. Once, Angela didn't come back home, so the foster mother took it out on me. She punched me in my mouth. She expected me to cry and not hit her back. But I punched her back in her mouth. I don't know how she got to be a foster mother.

The above quote illustrates the resentment children feel in substitute family settings. So while some parents want stricter discipline, children clearly do not. The very difficult role which the foster carers have to perform is also reflected.

Some children felt the material standards of foster homes to be low, and therefore issues of concern. One child repeatedly mentioned that his foster carer only had a small black-and-white television and no video. It is essential to recognize that the social, economic and political disadvantages experienced by black people in general also affect the black foster care community. This means that black children may be placed in homes where the material standards are relatively low.

Children who had had experience of residential establishments expressed their dissatisfaction of these settings. Their views echoed the arguments put forward elsewhere (CRE 1979, BIC 1984). Children complained about the unmet dietary needs and skin care as well as the general ignorance and attitude of the staff in children's homes. Some children explained how in their previous children's home, 'rice and peas' meant boiled rice and green peas, and not the traditional Caribbean rice and peas. Also, although Wenford had recruited greater numbers of black residential staff, children stated that very often homes only comprised one or two black members of staff. These initiatives were nevertheless perceived by some children to be positive aspects.

> *Child*: There were two friendly workers, Janet and David. I liked Janet because she cooked food like my mum's. The other staff just cooked other food which I didn't like. All the kids were black. There weren't any whites or Indians.

Since the Wenford research did not focus on residential institutions as subjects of study, it is not possible to state whether black children were more likely to be represented in certain homes in the borough than others. Interviews with children revealed that they often felt that the homes were full of black children. Since a great majority of the black children were placed in foster family settings, and the proportion of white children in residential homes was higher than that of black children, it can only be inferred that social workers used some children's homes to a greater degree for black children than others.

## Summary and conclusion

This chapter has explored the various issues related to the care process. As well as quantitatively documenting the placement pathways and destinations of children, it has been possible to explore the perceptions of parents and children about their experience of placement settings. The higher representation of black children in family settings was clearly one of the major findings on which this study has been able to shed light. The particular situation of Mixed-Origin, West African, Asian and Turkish Cypriot children has been discussed together with the light that this casts upon the workings of an idealistically 'ethnically sensitive' policy, combined with forms of worker sensitivity and resistance.

# 5

# *Rehabilitation and discharge*

This chapter discusses the process of rehabilitation and discharge of children from the care of the Social Services Department into their natural families and into the community. Although the two terms, rehabilitation and discharge, are generally used loosely and interchangeably, an important distinction is drawn in this study. Thus the chapter is divided along these two lines. Section one explores the process of rehabilitation while section two addresses the situation of children discharged from care.

The process of rehabilitation, for the purposes of this study, is defined as the facilitating of a situation to enable a child's return to his or her natural family. It is distinguished from the stage of discharge, in that discharge refers to the total departure from care (both legally and physically) while rehabilitation means that although the child has returned home, he/she is still legally in the care of the local authority. Discharge from care can take place via a number of routes. These can range from adoption, return to natural family/community upon reaching the age of 18 or 19 or upon discharge from accommodation (formerly voluntary care), or upon successful revocation of court order.

## *Section One*
## *Process of rehabilitaion*

The eventual aim of a local authority Social Services Department is to work towards the rehabilitation of children received in their care. This duty is actually enshrined in the legislation. At the time of this research and prior to the 1989 Children Act, for example, in the case of voluntary admissions, the law required that the social services shall 'in all cases where it appears to them consistent with the welfare of the child to do so, endeavour to ensure that the care of the child is taken over either by a parent or guardian, or ... relative' (Child Care Act 1980. S.2(3)).

The process of rehabilitation is influenced by a number of factors which stem from the child's experiences in care. Factors such as the length of time in care, parental contact, social worker contact and efforts made by the Social Services Department determine children's chances of rehabilitation (Millham et al 1986, Vernon and Fruin 1986). These factors were explored by the Wenford study and the findings are presented below.

## Length of time in care

Two recent studies which observed the factors which determine children's length of stay in care have come to similar conclusions (Millham et al 1986, Vernon and Fruin 1986). Millham et al (1986) found that if a child remains in care for longer than five weeks, he/she has a very strong chance (two out of three cases) of still being in care two years later. What efforts do social workers make to facilitate the process of rehabilitation? In their study of 11 local authorities, Vernon and Fruin (1986) found that once a child had been admitted into care, social workers accorded little priority to the case. Moreover, they argue that planning is not seen as a matter of concern by the social workers as time progresses.

The Wenford findings show that the majority of the cohort group had been in care for two or more years. A quarter of the children had been in care for more than ten years. No significant differences were found in the proportions of black and white children in these categories. A small proportion of the children had been in care for more than 15 years, of these the majority were black (72 per cent compared to 28 per cent white). Bearing in mind the findings of Millham et al, it could be argued that the chances for the majority of the children in the cohort group who had been in care for more than a year were reduced to a minimum.

## Parental links

The maintenance of good parental links is perceived to be a necessary prerequisite to exit from care. Studies done in the area of separation and loss highlight the importance of parent/child links (Holman 1966,

Stevenson 1968, Berry 1972). Millham et al (1986) have argued that the maintenance of close contact with their families is the best indicator that a child will leave local authority care rapidly.

In the Wenford study, parental contact was categorized as 'frequent', 'infrequent', and 'none' (see Chapter 2). 'Frequent' refers to contact (face to face or via letters, and telephone) which took place at least once per month. 'Infrequent' refers to contact which took place a few times a year, usually on birthdays, and Christmas Day. 'None' refers to where there was absolutely no contact at all. Due to the chaotic nature of social work case files, it was not possible to establish in this study whether contact had been terminated by the social services or had dissipated over time.

### (a) Parental links at the initial inquiry

Quite a sizeable proportion of the cohort had lost all contact with their natural families (one-third), while a similar proportion had only infrequent contact. Forty per cent of the cohort were found to have frequent contact with their natural families.

Differences were found to exist in terms of race. Black children had more frequent contact with their families than white children. With the exception of one area office (Area 4), this situation was in existence borough-wide. Where there was no contact at all, a greater proportion of white children than black children were found to exist (see Fig. 5.1).

### (b) Parental links at the follow-up inquiry

Six months after the initial inquiry, that is at the stage of follow-up, the level of parental contact was again measured to establish the change in circumstances. The pattern of parental links which was found to exist at the initial period of the study was very much in existence. That is, the level of frequent contact between black parents and black children was still greater than that between white parents and white children (see Fig. 5.2 in the Appendix).

### (c) Parental links by type of placement

An analysis of the level of parental contact and type of placement showed some interesting differences between black and white children.

*Figure 5.1    Parental links by race (%)*

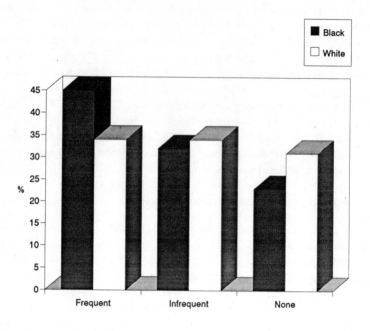

$\chi^2=8.230$        $p= <0.041$

## (i) Foster family

The findings presented in Figure 5.3 in the Appendix are highly statistically significant. Black children placed in foster families were much more likely to have frequent contact with their natural families than were white children placed in similar settings.

A comparison of same race and transracial placements showed that black children placed transracially had poor contact with their natural parents. We know from the previous chapter that a third of the black children had been placed transracially. Over 5 per cent of the children in this group had lost all contact with their families. Only 5 per cent had regular contact with their parents, and the remainder saw their parents occasionally. A reverse situation existed in the case of black children placed in black families. Over 50 per cent had regular contact with their parents, and only less than a fifth had lost all contact.

### (ii) Children's Homes

Of the children placed in Children's Homes, no significant difference was found to exist between black and white children. Only a small proportion in each of the two groups had lost all contact with their natural families (see Table 5.1 in the Appendix).

### (iii) Relatives

The majority of the children placed with relatives had some contact with their natural parents. Black children were found to have greater frequent contact than white children (see Table 5.2 in the Appendix).

### (d) Parental links by legal status

The legal status often determines the access arrangements between parents and children. In Chapter Three, it was found that the majority of black children were entering care via the voluntary route, but after a period of time in care they were as likely as white children to be made subject to compulsory care.

In an analysis of the legal status of children who had regular contact with their parents, it was found that of the black children about 50 per cent were in voluntary care and the other 50 per cent had either entered care via the compulsory route or had been made subject to compulsory care. Of the white children, the picture was not very different, about 40 per cent were in voluntary care while the other 60 per cent were subject to various forms of compulsory care. There were no significant proportional differences between black and white children.

Where there was no contact at all between parents and children, it was found that more than two-thirds (72 per cent) were in compulsory care, either made subject to a parental rights resolution (46 per cent), care order (39 per cent) or wardship (15 per cent). Black and white children were equally likely to be in this situation.

## *Social worker contact with natural family*

The degree of contact a social worker may have with the natural family plays an important part in the social services' decision to rehabilitate a child with his/her natural family. Social worker contact with natural family suggests that some kind of a relationship exists between the family and the Social Services Department, should rehabilitation be a matter of consideration.

The Wenford findings show that a very small proportion of social workers maintained contact with natural families following the admission of a child into care (7 per cent). The majority of the families had little or no contact at all with the social worker. It was found that there were no differences in terms of race, black and white families were equally likely to have a low level or no contact with their social worker.

The situation upon follow-up, six months after the initial study, did not differ greatly from that found in the initial inquiry. Very few natural families had regular contact with their social worker. There was little difference between black and white families in terms of their contact with the social worker (see Table 5.3 in the Appendix).

## Home on Trial attempts

Home on Trial attempts are a good indication of social work intervention to enable a child's rehabilitation into his/her natural family in the possibility that total discharge may occur. The attempts measured in this study related to both the current care episode and previous care episodes. This is because it was felt that previous attempts made by Wenford Social Services Department could not be ignored. For this reason, the proportions of children for whom Home on Trial was a possibility may seem high.

An attempt to place the child Home on Trial was made in about a third of all cases in the cohort group. In one area office (Area 4), rehabilitation attempts had only been made in about 15 per cent of the cases.

White children were much more likely to be rehabilitated than black children. This difference is quite pronounced in Area 2 and Area 4. In Area 2, for example, Home on Trial attempts had been made with 35 per cent of the white children compared with only 19 per cent of the black children (see Table 5.4 in the Appendix). The reasons for this difference are analysed later in the discussion.

*Section Two*
*Discharge from care*

Discharge from care refers to the complete departure, both legally and physically, from local authority care. This may occur in the form of adoption, discharge from accommodation, and revocation of a court order.

## Children discharged from care

Since this study was concerned with the care careers of children, the situation of the children in the cohort group was examined six months after the initial inquiry. Table 5.5 in the Appendix refers to all children in the cohort group. It shows the proportion who were discharged, and those who were still in care.

It should be noted that although more black children were discharged from care, their overall proportion in care was still higher than that of white children (51 per cent black compared with 49 per cent white). Moreover, they were still disproportionately represented in care.

## Length of time between admission and discharge

It is important to determine the period of time a child has spent in care before being discharged. An understanding of this factor shows whether children spend long periods in care or whether they are discharged from care as quickly as possible.

The Wenford findings show that over a fifth of the black children and a similar proportion of the white children left care within a year of being admitted (see Table 5.6 in the Appendix).

Those who left care after a period of between one and two years in care were predominantly black children. The majority of both black and white children were discharged after two or more years in care (75 per cent white, 58 per cent black).

It was found that sixteen of the children discharged from care were those from the sub-group who had come into care in the previous six months. The majority of these children were black (13 were black compared to only 3 who were white), and from one area office (Area 2).

Black children were nevertheless still disproportionately represented in the sub-group (66 per cent of the children were black compared to 34 per cent white).

## Routes of discharge from care

The two major exit routes were discharge from voluntary care (accommodation), and the attainment of adulthood. Of the black children who left care, the majority were withdrawn from voluntary care by their parents. On the other hand, the majority of the white children who left care had done so by virtue of age, that is, upon reaching the age of 18 or 19 when the local authority no longer had any responsibility to keep them in care. Very few children left care by any other means. Only one child out of 87, who left care, had rights and duties rescinded, and only two had a care order revoked. Of the children who left care by means of adoption (a total of five), all were white (see Table 5.7 below).

Table 5.7   Route of exit by race (%)

| Route of exit | Black | White | (number) |
|---|---|---|---|
| Adoption | 0 | 11 | (5) |
| Age 18/19 | 40 | 55 | (47) |
| CO discharged | 2 | 3 | (2) |
| R & D rescinded | 0 | 3 | (1) |
| Vol. care discharged | 58 | 28 | (45) |
| Total (%) (n) | 100 (47) | 100 (36) | 100 (83) |

$\chi^2 = 12.807$ p$= < 0.012$

## Place of residence after leaving care

It was found that the majority of the children who left care had returned to their natural families (about one-third). The remainder, who were all over 18 years of age, either had their own accommodation in the form of a bed-sitter or flat, or they were living in hostels.

The proportion of black children returning to live with their natural families was slightly higher than white children, while the proportion of white children who went into 'other' type of accommodation was slightly higher than black children. It is instructive to note that the category 'other' in this instance includes those white children who went into adoptive families, hence the difference between black and white groups since no black child was adopted.

There were no differences found in terms of race in the age groups of children who returned to their families. Adolescents were just as likely to return to their families as were younger children. The results in the table below show that race as a factor was not predictive of significant differences in rates of transition into any of the three exit categories.

Table 5.8   Place of residence upon leaving care by race (%)

| Place of residence | Black | White | Total | (n) |
|---|---|---|---|---|
| Natural Family | 63 | 58 | 60 | (46) |
| Own accommodation | 21 | 21 | 21 | (16) |
| Other (Hostel, B&B etc) | 16 | 21 | 19 | (14) |
| Total (%) (n) | 100 (43) | 100 (33) | 100 | (76) |

$\chi^2 = 0.647$ p = $< 0.723$

## Discussion and analysis

The dearth of research evidence in this area prevents a comparative analysis. As the previous chapters have shown most studies have preoccupied themselves with particular aspects of the admission and placement of black children. There is virtually no information available in the area of rehabilitation and discharge. This chapter discusses the findings of the research in the light of the paucity of information in this area.

Research studies which have focused on some of the relevant issues have tended to adopt a definition of rehabilitation and discharge which is incongruent with the one adopted in this study (Rowe and Lambert 1973, ABSWAP 1983). These studies have taken rehabilitation and discharge to mean removal from institutional care into either natural or substitute family. This study has defined rehabilitation and discharge as placement with natural parents, or guardians, and adoption or return into the community where the child has his/her own accommodation. Thus placement within foster family settings has not been taken to mean rehabilitation or discharge. However, the placement of children within adoptive families is perceived as discharge from care, since the local authority no longer has any legal responsibility.

In their evidence to the House of Commons, ABSWAP (1983) asserted that in one London borough in a sample of 100 children (50 black, 50 white) who came into care within the same period, after six months there were clear differences in the patterns of rehabilitation. In the white group, the proportion of children remaining in institutions was likely to be reduced by 60 per cent. In the black group by contrast, the proportion of children was likely to be reduced by only 20 per cent. Thus the chances of black children being rehabilitated into their natural families or substitute families were greatly reduced. Similarly, Rowe and Lambert (1973) in their nationwide study found that one in five of the children in their sample were black. They argued that because of the difficulty in finding substitute family placements, black children were spending longer periods in care, where care was taken to mean institutional care only.

Although the findings of the above two studies are useful, they cannot be readily compared with the findings of the Wenford research because of the difference in focus and definition. Had the Wenford study adopted the definition of these particular studies, it would have been shown that black children were more likely to be rehabilitated than white children since the findings demonstrate that there were more black children being placed in foster family settings.

Level of contact between natural parents and children is a crucial contributory factor leading to the rehabilitation and discharge of children from care. The Wenford study showed that a greater proportion of black children than white children had regular contact with their parents. The situation boroughwide was such that 45 per cent of the black children had regular contact with their parents compared with only 34 per cent of the white children. Where there was no contact at all, the majority of the children and families were white. This contact had either been terminated on legal grounds by the SSD, or parents and children had lost contact over the years.

As in the cohort group, the sub-group also showed that black parents were more likely than white parents to have regular contact with their children. This contact was almost always initiated by parents themselves. Most black parents saw their children twice a week, while the contacts between white parents and children were beginning to wither away.

> *White Child*: My mom doesn't come as often as she used to. She has work to do, she has kids to look after.

> *White Parent*: I don't go to see him because it's upsetting, coming home without him.

White parents often had little idea of where their child was placed. This suggested that they had very rarely visited their child. Also, in their view, a few visits a year were sufficient contact.

> *White Mother*: He's placed in a foster family somewhere in the north of Wenford, I think. We'll be going to see him at Christmas of course, take his Christmas present and that. It'll be his first Christmas away from us. I mean I do see him at birthdays, Christmas and that.

What role did social workers play in encouraging contact between parents and children? A recent study (Vernon and Fruin 1986) found that:

> Parent-child contact was not a feature relayed by social workers as of importance in relation to placement ... Social workers invariably commented that they left this (visiting arrangements) to be worked out between the foster parents and the parent.

(Vernon and Fruin 1986, as quoted in DHSS 1985:10–11)

Although the above study did not focus upon the 'race dimension', its findings are remarkably similar to the Wenford study, which found that after the initial admission into care, while some social workers explored the possibilities of encouraging contact between parents and children, most social workers did not see this as a matter of concern. Indeed, parental contact was often seen as being good for the parent and not necessarily for the child. Also, as the cohort findings show social worker themselves had very minimal contact with the natural parents after the stage of admission. Workers often accepted the diminishing contact as a normal state of affairs over which they had no control:

> *Social Worker*: She doesn't visit the child. She used to.

> *Social Worker*: The mother has disappeared from the scene. We have been unable to trace her. Keith is still in voluntary care.

> *Social Worker*: Mother visited very irregularly. Her attendance at family meetings also left a lot to be desired.

> *Social Worker*: Her visits haven't in any way been encouraged. She's just left to her own devices. We've deliberately kept a low profile.

Vernon and Fruin (1986) demonstrated the social workers' propensity to adopt a neutral stance. They argue:

> In general, the effects of their so-called 'neutral' stance were unrecognizesed and when, according to them, they were exercising no influence on a case, they were, in fact, creating obstacles to children returning home ... the significance of maintaining contact between children and their parents received little attention or priority.

(Vernon and Fruin 1986:147)

The Wenford study found ample evidence of this neutral stance adopted by social workers. Moreover, it was also found that far from fostering contact between parents and children some social workers demonstrated their power over clients by creating barriers. Little was done to facilitate links. Parents often saw themselves being put through extremes as a test of their commitment to their child. In the case of a one year old white baby admitted into care for failure to thrive, and now on a care order and placed with a foster family, the social worker objected to the father wanting to visit on a particular day of the week because she did not work that day of the week.

*Social Worker*: The father wanted to visit on Wednesdays because it fitted in with his work. But I mean if the foster mother needed help, I would not be there to turn to on Wednesdays.

It appears that in the case of both black and white families, social worker attitudes towards encouraging parental links with the child as well as maintaining social worker contact with the family do not differ a great deal. Also, social workers are themselves very unlikely to maintain contact with natural families after the stage of admission. Little or no attempt is made to ensure any form of contact between the child and the family.

If social workers expect natural parents and foster carers to negotiate the visiting arrangements as was found by Vernon and Fruin (1986), what then is the situation regarding natural parents and foster parents in terms of race? The Wenford study findings show that black children placed in foster families, particularly black foster families, were more likely than white children to have regular contact with their parents. Black children placed in transracial foster families were found to have lost all contact with their natural parents.

The placement of black children in black families is obviously an important factor in terms of access. Almost all black foster families were from within the same borough. This undoubtedly led to better links being maintained between black parents and children. There were several cases of black children who were placed with a foster mother only a 'few streets away'. Furthermore, black foster carers operated an 'open house' policy whereby very few if any restrictions were imposed upon parents visiting their children. Black foster carers made no objections to the disclosure of their address and telephone number to natural parents. This 'open house' practice was less likely to be found in the case of white foster carers. The following quotes illustrate this difference in approach. It is important to understand that such an approach often determined the level of contact between parents and children placed in substitute settings.

In the case of black children and parents:

*Social Worker*: Mother keeps in touch with the foster mother and vice versa, via telephone.

*Social Worker*: At the moment, mother is having 48 hours contact with Sandra and John (the children). She picks them up on a Friday, and drops them off on Sunday. Sometimes, this is extended by prior arrangement with the foster mother.

93

In the case of white children and parents:

*Social Worker*: Mother visits too frequently, and too irregularly for the foster mother's liking. This has been the cause of much friction.

*Social Worker*: Child visits her parents on a regular basis. They don't visit her because the foster parent's address is confidential.

*Social Worker*: We placed the girls with foster parents. The foster parents were rejecting mother's visits and taking the attitude that she was as guilty as the father.

The need to keep the foster carers' address confidential is sometimes necessary especially in situations where children are considered to be at risk. However, all the above cases refer to children admitted into voluntary care except in the last quote where the children were admitted into care following allegations of sexual abuse and made wards of court. In the visiting arrangements in these cases, there was no immediate danger of the children being at risk. Interviews with social workers, parents and children revealed that friction between the foster carers and natural parents often led to diminished contact.

In situations where children were placed in residential establishments, it was found that while children in the borough's own homes were more likely to have contact with their parents, children placed in Community Homes (CHEs) outside the borough were in danger of losing contact with their parents. Social workers did not always see this as a matter of concern. If social workers opposed out of borough placements, it was usually on the grounds that it was going to be difficult to monitor the case. Some social workers described such homes as holiday homes set in beautiful countryside which would do the children a 'lot of good':

Social Worker: I mean if you see it, you fall in love with it. It's a really nice place. It's like a bungalow, you know, your own place.

It was argued by social workers that, generally speaking, children saw their parents at weekends only. Thus it was felt that this type of weekend contact was possible even if the children were placed in locations such as Norwich or Dorset. Social workers asserted that it took just as long to travel across London. There was relatively little understanding or concern about the uprooting of children.

*Social Worker*: The future plan is to find a Community Home with education on the premises. We don't have any in Wenford. We'd have to place him in Norwich or Bristol.

The presence of black staff in residential homes within the borough is a positive factor in terms of maintaining family links. It was without a doubt a contributory factor in giving black parents the confidence to make regular visits to their children. For the purposes of this study, it was possible to visit a few of the homes outside the borough. These homes, particularly in places such as Norwich and Dorset, had a very eurocentric atmosphere. The following quote by a black social worker about a black child in voluntary care, placed in a CHE outside the borough illustrates this point:

> *Social Worker*: There weren't any black kids when she first went there. There are two now. There is only one black member of care staff, the other is a cleaner. There is no work done on the children's racial identity. The place is very white.

So not only did the geographical distance jeopardize parental links, but black children felt totally alienated in an environment far removed from their neighbourhood and communities. The difficulties young black people face upon returning to their own communities after years in such institutions are enormous (BIC 1984). The problems faced by black youngsters in general upon leaving care in terms of employment and accommodation have been explored elsewhere (First Key 1987, Garnett 1992).

Millham et al (1986) in their study of 450 children conclude that the maintenance of close contact with their families is the best indicator that a child will leave local authority care rapidly. The Wenford study findings show that this may be true for white children, but it was not the case for black children. It was found that although black children had better links with their parents than did white children, they were less likely to experience being placed Home on Trial. Could it be that social workers have less confidence in placing black children Home on Trial? Interviews with social workers certainly attested to this.

> *Social Worker*: The staff at Lynford House were arguing very strongly that Richard and his mom should be forced to go back with each other. They were arguing that the longer Richard was in care, the worse it was for Richard and his mom, and that there was no reason for Richard to be in care.

The above quote refers to the case first mentioned in Chapter Three. Richard, a 15-year-old African-Caribbean boy initially entered voluntary care after having stolen from his mother's purse. Other problems of delinquency came to light after Richard's reception into care. This resulted in Richard being made subject to a care order. His initial placement was in an Observation and Assessment centre, where he spent six months because no other placement could be found for him. After this period, he was temporarily placed in one of the borough's own homes while arrangements were made to find a suitable CHE placement for him somewhere out of the borough. It was while Richard was in this home, that conflict developed between the white field social worker and the black residential staff. The ultimate power of the field social worker is demonstrated here. Richard was not rehabilitated with his mother as suggested by the black residential staff, but sent to a CHE outside the borough.

An analysis of the white children placed Home on Trial showed that the majority were adolescents, admitted into care for reasons of delinquency, and sometimes placed Home on Trial from the very beginning. That is, although they were technically in care, they had never physically entered care. There were black children who were in a similar situation as these children, but they did not follow the same path as them.

The cohort study found that the proportion of black children discharged from care was slightly higher than that of white children (17 per cent black and 13 per cent white). The routes by which these children left care was interesting. It was clear that social services were not instrumental in the discharge of children. Most children were either withdrawn from care by their parents, or they left care upon reaching the age of 18 or 19 when the social services no longer had any responsibility for them. The fact that more black children left care within two years of admission is undoubtedly due to their legal status in care. The majority were discharged from voluntary care. White children's compulsory care status ensured their longer stay in care. Due to the very passive role adopted by social workers, children remained in care particularly when their legal status was statutory. In the case of white children, however, Home on Trial placements were a useful indicator of some active work on the part of the social workers.

A low level or non-existent contact between social workers and natural families is an indicator of a social worker's apathetic role. Interviews with social workers revealed that discharge from care was something they very rarely contemplated. Remarks such as the following were commonplace:

*Social Worker*: I think once the children come into care, it's very difficult to get them back.

*Social Worker*: I don't know I've never discharged anyone from care.

Some social workers argued that although they were willing to discharge children from care, it was the natural parents who were reluctant to have their children back:

*Social Worker*: You get some parents, who once the kids are in care, they don't want to co-operate with you. They don't want to visit their children. They don't want to get involved in the rehabilitation pro- gramme. So it's this thing about 'you can't send my children home to me, because I haven't got accommodation. I can't cope, I can't do this, I can't do that'.

The poor socio-economic situation of black parents which was often the contributory factor for the admission of a black child into care played an important part in social worker decisions to rehabili- tate and discharge children. For example, if there was no change in the parents' socio-economic circumstances, it was unlikely that a child would be returned home. Thus the parents' poor situation coupled with negative social worker attitudes ensured the child's stay in care. The following quote regarding a West African father illus- trates this point. The social worker explains why the children have remained in care on a long-term basis.

*Social Worker*: Mr Atolagbe was wanting to take the children back, made every effort to have the children back, but he lived in terrible circum- stances, two cramped damp attic rooms, cooker on the landing, and other kitchen facilities cramped in one room with beds in it as well. So they remained in care.

As discussed in Chapter Three, there was a clear difference between the perceptions of parents and social workers. In some instances, the standards adopted by social workers conflicted with those of parents. These ranged from material circumstances as outlined in the above quotation to interpersonal relationships. Some parents argued that they wished to have their child back, but stated the child had changed his/her mind about going back home. Parents felt angry that the social worker was siding with the child and hindering all prospects of a good relationship between them and their child.

Parents, both black and white, whose children were in compulsory care were fully aware of the statutory implications. This finding contradicts a recent study conducted in Sheffield by Fisher et al (1986) which stated that parents were not particularly concerned about the implications of compulsory care. This difference in finding can be explained by the fact that the Sheffield study focused on adolescent children who were admitted for reasons such as delinquency and behavioural problems, circumstances of which parents and social workers had common understanding. This study consisted of a cohort of children of all ages who were admitted into care for a multiplicity of reasons. Thus it was not biased towards any particular group of children. This diversity naturally meant that in the Wenford study there were parents who did not share a common definition of the underlying problems with social workers.

There were parents who felt powerless, but created the impression that they would be fighting against the decision of the Social Services Department:

> *Mother*: I've got a very good solicitor and barrister. You see, social services want to try and make out it is better for the children to remain in care. One day, there was a school progress report for Kathy which was delivered to this address. I opened it and it was an awful report. My solicitor has made copies of this for the court hearing. We've also made copies of school reports for the period before Kathy was taken into care. These 'before reports' are much better. So we'll try and fight the case on this issue. Also, we've got letters from the girls saying they want to come home.

> *Mother*: At the moment, we're taking the social services to court for what they've done.

Parents were aware of the fact the local authority was in control, and that although they had some contact with their child the situation was tenuous. They realised that discharge from care was not something upon which they had a great deal of influence.

In Chapter Three, it was highlighted that the majority of the families in the cohort group had been known to the social services for many years. In interviews with parents it was learnt that years of involvement with the social services had created disillusionment and dissatisfaction in them. Many felt that nothing positive had come out of their involvement and in a way they regretted ever having contacted the social services. Most of the black parents whose children were admitted into voluntary care initially came to the Social Service

Department seeking help and advice, unaware of the full implications of their actions and with hindsight, stated that they should not have approached the social services.

> *Mother*: This place is really overcrowded, the bedrooms are really small, and I have four children, two in each of the two bedrooms. I've been asking for a transfer for the past five years. Nothing's been done. Social services won't do anything. Yet, when they want to, they do, for example they didn't waste any time in taking my kids into care.

Many black parents stated that poor housing had been their major problem, and felt very strongly that social workers had not adequately advocated on their behalf. Some white parents of adolescent children also felt that they had not gained the advice they sought. They often felt blamed for their child's behaviour.

Both black and white parents felt that although they had been given practical help, social workers had not been able to detect the root of their problem. One mother stated that her main problems had been marital discord and alcoholism. While she had been able to obtain an injunction to keep her husband away from the house, alcoholism which was one of her major problems was never detected by any of her social workers. In fact, one of her social workers used to go drinking with her.

The majority of the parents interviewed, both black and white, expressed their dissatisfaction with the social services. They pinned no hope in the social workers. With respect to the discharge of their children, they gave the impression of being completely helpless whether their children were in voluntary or compulsory care.

In the Wenford research, it was found that after leaving care, the majority of children went to live with their natural families. Two-thirds of these children were black. It could be that because there are better links between black children and families, that the proportion of black children returning to natural families is higher. Another significant factor is that many black children were withdrawn from voluntary care by their parents.

A third of the children who left care did not return to their natural families, but found their own accommodation such as bed-sitters, flats, or a place in a hostel. The majority of the white children who left care were over the age of 18. This meant that very often, they received the help of the social worker to find their own accommodation.

## Summary and conclusion

In this chapter, it has been possible to illustrate some of the factors influencing the process of rehabilitation and discharge. The findings of the sub-group were used to analyse and discuss the situation presented by the cohort group. Unfortunately, there is insufficient previous research literature on black children to make a comparative analysis. Nevertheless, the comparisons made with some of the mainstream studies on white children's rehabilitation and discharge patterns have proved to be useful.

One of the salient findings of this research was that although there was good contact between black children and parents, black children were in fact less likely to be placed Home on Trial than white children. It was also found that the very reason for the black children's greater contact with their parents was the fact that they were placed in black foster families. Black children in transracial families did not experience the same degree of regular contact as those in same race placements.

Although more black children than white left the care system, they were still significantly over-represented. Moreover, the route of exit for the majority of these children was withdrawal from voluntary care. The role of social workers in these withdrawals was very limited.

# 6

# *A different reality: black and white child care careers*

The extent to which black families and children receive a qualitatively poor service has been shown in previous chapters. Although social work practice, provision and policy is far from perfect in the case of white families, it is clear that issues of race and ethnicity predominate in a reductionist manner against the interests of black clients. This chapter attempts to integrate the major findings of this study. Whilst discussing the care career process in the light of the similarities and differences found to exist between black and white groups, an analysis is made to conceptualize and contextualize the salient findings. Theoretical and practice issues are intertwined to provide a thorough examination of the care career process. Major findings stemming from this study are listed below.

## *Major findings*

1. A great majority of the families had previous involvement with social services (80 per cent). About 50 per cent of the cohort group had been in care on previous occasions. However, only a small minority had several previous care episodes.

2. An overwhelming majority of children (74 per cent) were from single parent families. These one parent families were, on the whole, mother headed units (89 per cent). The proportion of black children (83 per cent) coming from single parent families was significantly higher than that of white children (64 per cent).

3. Black children were much more likely than white children to come from higher socio-economic groups. For example, 47 per cent of the black children's mothers were in white-collar and skilled-manual occupations compared to 22 per cent of white children.

4. The majority of families lived in local authority housing (93 per cent).

5. Both black boys and girls were disproportionately represented in the care system in comparison to their proportion in the general child population. Such over-representation was not specific to any one age group. Furthermore, disproportional representation was found to exist in all four area offices in the borough of Wenford.

6. Black children's route of entry into care differed significantly from that of white children. The majority of the black children entered care under Section 2 of the 1980 Child Care Act, that is, their legal status was voluntary.

7. There were qualitative differences in the social work help employed in the early stages of referral and admission. Social workers were less likely to engage black families than white families in preventative work to obviate children's admission into care.

8. The police were more likely to refer black children than white children for delinquency.

9. The health service was more likely to refer cases of black mothers than white mothers for reasons of mental health.

10. While there were some similarities, black and white children entered care for different reasons. For example, most black children entered care for reasons of socio-economic difficulties, family relationships, and mother's mental health, while most white children entered care for parental neglect/inadequacy, failure to thrive, child abuse, delinquency, non-school attendance and child's behaviour.

11. Black children were admitted into care twice as quickly as white children after the initial referral date.

12. Although black children entered care on a voluntary basis, once in care they were as likely as white children to be made subject to compulsory care. In fact, black children were much more likely to be made subject to a parental rights resolution than white children.

13. Black children had a much better chance of being placed in a foster family than white children. Moreover, these placements were in racially and culturally appropriate families.

14. No differences were found to exist between black and white children in the total number of placements whilst in care. These were calculated from all care episodes.

15. Black children enjoyed a more regular level of parental contact than white children.

16. Black children placed in black foster families had a much higher

chance of maintaining contact with their natural families. Those placed in white substitute families had little or no contact with their natural parents.

17. Both black and white families and children had minimal social worker contact after admission into care.

18. Although more black children left care as a result of either parents resuming care, or children attaining adulthood, they were less likely than white children to be placed Home on Trial.

## The significance of race

This study documents, in very cogent terms, that while there are some similarities, on the whole black and white children lead different paths in their care careers. Interviews with social workers, natural parents and children provided some explanations for these differences. The role of social work theory and ideology and its influence on social work practice needs careful consideration. Moreover, social work professionalism, departmental policies and provision, and the political and ideological significance of race as a concept are useful in understanding the processes which militate discriminatory practices against black families and children.

An examination of the role of state social work is important here. Gramscian or other neo-Marxist approaches are often deemed appropriate as frameworks for understanding the role of the personal social services and the ways in which hegemonic control is maintained over the lives of families and children who come into contact with them (Bailey and Brake 1975, Corrigon and Leonard 1978, Statham 1978). Although these analyses are useful in understanding the state apparatus in the sphere of social work, they provide inadequate conceptualization of the differences found between black and white groups in this study. In the light of Wenford findings which suggest that race as a variable plays a crucial role in the way the state responds to the needs of individuals, we need to recognize the correlation between race and hegemonic control. An understanding of economic, political, and ideological discourse on race becomes essential to appreciate the processes at work. A recognition of the ways in which structures operate to issues of race, via institutional, individual and cultural racism culminating in discriminatory practices to the detriment of black people in this society is absolutely necessary (Dominelli 1988).

Previous research has documented the disproportionate representation of black children in the public care system. While the numbers of black children in care have been expressed as a cause for concern, very little structural analysis is drawn about their disproportionate representation. Explanations such as family structures, values and beliefs, and higher birth rates in the black community are unsatisfactory, and serve to pathologize black family life (Fitzherbert 1967, Foren and Batta 1970, Batta, McCulloch and Smith 1975, McCulloch, Batta and Smith 1979, Boss and Homeshaw 1974). Explanations from a disadvantage/deprivation perspective provide some understanding, but they are too deeply embedded in the orthodox class analysis model (Pinder and Shaw 1974, Lambeth 1981). The Wenford findings show that black families were more likely to come from higher socio-economic backgrounds than were white families; this suggests that we need to move beyond the disadvantage and social class analysis if we are to begin to understand the experiences of black families and children in the personal social services. While recognizing the limited powers of the social services and the constraints within which they operate, we need to examine the ways in which social services respond to problems presented by black families and children.

In an examination of social work case files and in interviews with social workers and natural parents, it became apparent that preventive work was less likely to be done with black families (Barn 1990). Considering that the majority of black children entered care via the voluntary route, this posed some interesting questions. Why are black children admitted into care at twice the speed of white children? Are the problems of black families perceived to be insurmountable? If so, why? Are social workers ill-equipped to help alleviate black families' problematic situations? The voluntary nature of black admissions suggests that most families either presented themselves or they were referred by other agencies to the social services with problems which required preventative action. Social services were under a duty to ameliorate difficulties being faced by these parents to obviate the need to receive the child or children into care.

The Wenford study demonstrates the difference in social services response to black and white families. In the case of a black family where a six year old child was in care, the social work case file had the following note attached to the front cover:

> Julie is presently saying she does not want anything to do with me – so hopefully she will not be in contact making any demands.

Julie demanded financial assistance, on my refusal she threatened:
(a) She will have to go out to steal and we will have to take her kids into care.
(b) She will bring her children down here if she's not given any money.
NO MONEY SHOULD BE GIVEN UNDER ANY CIRCUM-STANCES – SEND TO DHSS.

The above example illustrates an inflexible and a traditional Victorian approach to social work problems in its entrenched belief of distinguishing between 'deserving' and 'non-deserving' poor. The above case points to the failure of one aspect of preventative work, that is, the provision of financial assistance. Other types of preventative work, for example, assistance with housing, welfare benefits, family relationships, counselling, and day care were also less likely to be employed in the case of black families. The professional ideologies of social workers led them to view problems of families in an individualistic and parochial manner. Black parents were perceived as anti-authority and hostile, and social workers found it difficult to work with them. This had disastrous consequences. Thus not only were preventative strategies less likely to be employed with black families in the early stages of admission into care but the consequences of this were far reaching and subsequently affected other aspects of a child's care career.

As already mentioned, not only were black children disproportionately represented in care, they were also more likely to be admitted into care sooner than white children. The following case illustrates the readiness of social services to take black children into voluntary care:

## David

David, a 16-year-old West African boy presented himself to Wenford social services. He stated that his mother was in Nigeria, and that his father had died. He had moved from Manchester where he had lived with his friends, and was now homeless. The social services received him into care. He was placed with a black foster family. The social worker described him as 'a bright young lad who was studying for his A levels'. After about 12 months in care, it was discovered that the whole case had been a fraud. The boy was not 16 but 21. He had lived

105

in Wenford for some years and had his own flat. The police were said to be investigating the case.

The above example is atypical, but it does show that social services are extremely hasty in receiving black children into care. In another case, a white mother had enormous difficulty in trying to persuade the social services to take her 16-year-old son into care despite her pleas that he was violent towards her. The response of the social services was that she was his parent and guardian and therefore responsible for him. The boy was finally admitted into care as a result of care proceedings initiated by the mother who was knowledgeable about the law having been a social worker herself. There is a sharp contrast in the response of the social services in these two cases. In the case of the black child, admission into care took place without any questions being asked. In the case of the white child, the social services were adamant not to pursue an admission. The white child was admitted into care not as a result of the social services efforts, but because the mother successfully managed to achieve her aim. In both cases the social services were doing a disservice to the families. Social workers' tendency to intervene in the case of black families without making adequate assessments and offering appropriate support invariably results in the greater admissions of black children into care.

In view of the fact that the majority of black admissions into care were of a voluntary nature, one needs to examine the voluntary aspect of this concept. The *Oxford Dictionary* defines voluntary as 'performed or done of one's own free will, impulse, or choice'. Black people as victims of institutional, individual and cultural racism are the most disadvantaged group in society (PEP 1967, Smith 1977, Brown 1984). The chances of them needing help and assistance in the areas of housing, employment, education, social security, immigration, and social services are therefore greater. It is because of their poor circumstances that they would call upon the social services for help. The concept of voluntary bears little relevance to the situation. Their deprivation and disadvantage forces them to seek the help of welfare agencies. The agencies which are designed to assist fail to recognize the onslaught of racism upon the lives of black clients and in fact, by design or default, contribute to the perpetuation of such a situation.

Social services in Britain carry the Victorian legacy of helping those who help themselves. Thus, problems are invariably viewed in an individualistic manner. There is little or no appreciation of the structures which create situations of disadvantage and deprivation. In their failure to recognize and act upon the structural inequalities, social services remain reactive rather than proactive in promoting social and political change. The reluctance of British social work to engage in community work and action, and the eurocentric philosophies of social work methods such as psychoanalysis, behaviour modification, and family therapy are all testimony to the social services' limited understanding of needs and problems of black families and children. Introductory texts in social work describe methods of intervention, but do not offer a critical examination of these. For example, Coulshed's *Social Work Practice*, now a key text on social work courses, only recently incorporated feminist and anti-discriminatory perspectives (Coulshed 1992). However it does little more than pay lip service to these concepts, and fails to move beyond this. By defining problems in an individualistic and familial manner, the focus remains limited to particular strategies.

Fitzherbert (1967) in her study of African-Caribbean children in Lewisham recommended that social services ought to employ 'tough casework' in their work with African-Caribbean families. The problem was located within the family, it was the family which put the children into care. There is little appreciation of the disadvantaged situation of the family which may lead it to request help from the social services. Working within such a framework where it is the family which is seen as deviant there can be little hope for an understanding of the family's circumstances.

State social work tends to perpetuate oppressive social relations in its portrayal of the 'good family' as two parents, white, middle class, heterosexual and able-bodied. There is enormous veneration of this family unit, and the dichotomy of the 'good' and 'bad' parent is continually reinforced.

In the case of black families and children, pathological notions about family structures, their values and belief patterns have become part of the racial discourse (Carby 1982, Lawrence 1981). The ability and competence of black families to rear children is questioned in the context of this liberalist society. Black families are viewed very much within the assimilation/integration framework. Referrals from such families invariably result in an examination of family structure, and how it is supposedly jeopardizing the welfare of the child. Whilst one-parent families are perceived as inadequate for the upbringing of children in general, black one-parent families are perceived as especially deviant. In these situations, care is sometimes seen as a better alternative, and the 'rescue mentality' of the social services is particularly noticeable.

In this study, it was found that black children were not only likely to be admitted into care more quickly than white children in cases of socio-economic difficulties and family relationships, but also where allegations of child abuse had been made. Black cases of child abuse, for example, were less likely to be treated with an open mind than white cases. Social workers' negative views about black families led them to be unnecessarily cautious. In conjunction with other agencies, they tended to adopt a 'rescue mentality' and as a consequence over-reacted in these situations. This highly zealous crusading mission had enormous repercussions for black families and children. Black social workers felt that in some instances cases of 'mongolian blue spots' on black children were misdiagnosed as actual child physical abuse. In one such case, a black mother was charged with assault when it was argued that the 'right buttock had a much darker area of skin beneath the normal brown colouring'.

These situations had, to some extent, been heightened in the wake of two cases where black children had been killed at the hands of their parents and guardians (Jasmine Beckford 1985, Tyra Henry 1987). It has been asserted that because of these tragedies, social services were being extremely cautious (Hildrew 1986). Neill Kay, director of social services for Sheffield, maintains that children were being taken into care or kept there unnecessarily because of anxiety in social services departments after the inquiry into the death of Jasmine Beckford (Hildrew 1986). It is disturbing to note that in the borough of Wenford such cautious behaviour and action generally manifested itself in the case of black families.

The findings of this study suggest however that the experiences of black children in care were not entirely negative, and it would be wrong to assert that they were. Black children were more likely than white children to be placed in substitute family placements. Moreover, black children were being placed in racially and culturally appropriate families. Also, while the majority of black children were more likely than white children to have better parental links, black children placed in black substitute family settings were particularly likely to have better contact with their parents than those other black children placed in white substitute families.

Black children were found to have a better chance of being placed in a foster family. This finding is unique and contradicts previous general findings regarding the placement of black children (Rowe and Lambert 1973, Dale 1986). In the past, it has been found that black children are more likely to be placed in institutional care because of the difficulty in finding substitute families for them.

It is important to analyse the role played by the social services towards these positive outcomes. With respect to the placement aspect of child care careers, the differences between black and white children were found to be as a direct result of social services policy, provision and practice.

It would appear that the same race placement policy adopted by the borough of Wenford was more than mere rhetoric. The policy was backed by sufficient resources which made it possible for black children to be placed with black families. The role of black workers in the introduction and implementation of this policy was of crucial significance. It has to be noted that their contribution has been enormous in this area of work.

While on the whole, the outcome of the same-race placement policy has been positive, it is not without complications. The clear aims and objectives of the policy were not always matched by social work practice. For example, the situation of Mixed-Origin children was felt to be of particular concern by some social workers. These social workers were generally white but included some black social workers. Social work ideals such as 'client self-determination' and 'respect for the individual' were expressed to be lacking in the same-race placement policy. It was argued that it was wrong to select a black family in each case. The views of the mother (who was invariably white), and the Mixed-Origin child were said to be paramount.

A high proportion of the black children was placed in black families. These placements were found to be successful. There were good relationships between natural parents and children. Consequently, there were better links between children and natural parents. Parents were able to visit their children without the restrictions which can sometimes be applied by foster carers. Children placed trans-racially were found to have fewer links with their natural parents. Thus the same situation was not in existence where white foster carers and black natural parents were concerned. The study indicates, however, that better links between black parents and children were not as a result of the efforts made by social services, but due to the efforts made by parents and children themselves.

The borough of Wenford had by a policy decision closed down most of its children's homes. The homes which were in existence had undergone changes in recent years. The needs of black children were now on the agenda. The employment of black staff was perceived by many in the department as a step in the right direction.

It was interesting to note that whereas the importance of identity for Jewish children was a matter of concern, the same was not true for black children. Considerable attention was paid to the cultural and religious needs of Jewish children, for example, private Hebrew lessons were arranged and paid for by Wenford Social Services Department. Such incidents were unheard of in the case of black children. The assimilationist/integrationist ideology of the organization ensured the non-acceptance of religious, linguistic and cultural needs of black children.

The experiences of black children in institutional settings varied depending on the nature and location. Those children placed within the borough were able to have better links with their natural parents, relatives and the community compared to those placed in rural settings such as Norfolk and Suffolk. While the borough's homes had some black staff and catered for the needs of the black children to some extent, the homes in the rural settings were extremely eurocentric and alienating for the children. The implications of these placements were not fully understood by social workers.

The study shows that although the majority of black children entered care via the voluntary route, they were as likely as white children to be made subject to compulsory care. This, to some extent, jeopardized their chances of rehabilitation. However, we know that more white children entered compulsory care than black children, yet these white children had a much better chance of rehabilitation, in the form of Home on Trial. Also, although better links were maintained between black parents and children, this did not work in their interests.

The following examples of black and white children illustrate the differences in the response of the social services to the rehabilitation process.

Two white children, brother and sister (age 8 and 7 respectively), were admitted into care following allegations of sexual abuse. The stepfather and perpetrator was found guilty and sentenced to three years imprisonment. Both children had been in voluntary care once before. In 1983, after about 18 months in prison, the stepfather was released on parole. Five months later, in 1984, the two children were placed Home on Trial. A year later, the stepfather was again charged with unlawful sexual intercourse with the girl, and sent to prison for four years. Both of the children were again admitted into care. In 1987, the stepfather was released from prison. The social worker argued that the stepfather had received group therapy and psychiatric help on several occasions in the last six to seven years. It seemed as if the children would be returned home once more. Both children were in children's homes. For an organization that is designed to protect vulnerable children, this case exemplifies gross professional misjudgment.

In the case of a West African family, where the child was in care as a result of problematic family relationships, the social worker argued that the parents were uninterested in having their child back. Consequently, no attempts were made to rehabilitate the child. The social work file contained the following comment:

> Mr and Mrs Ameke pretend to be interested in their child but their interest is far from being genuine. Melanie does not seem to be fond of her parents and would very rarely make any mention of them. Rehabilitation is out of the question.

The child was placed with white foster carers and likely to remain there.

In the case of an Asian family, the children were received into care following a place of safety order, because the mother was found 'not to be discharging her parental duties'. That is, there was no food in the house, the mother was found to be drunk, and there was marital discord in the family. The social worker's pen picture of the mother read:

> Mrs Ahmed is of Asian origin, small, brown eyes, dark medium length hair, sallow complexion, dirty in appearance, with slurred speech often incoherent.

In the case of this family, the father had remarried. The social services perceived his new 27-year-old wife to be unsuitable to care for the children. It was argued that she 'had no previous experience with children, and did not speak English'. Also, although the father was described as having a fairly good relationship with the children, it was said that he saw his 'role more as a material provider rather than a parent who could give emotionally too'.

The above issues were discussed at the foster care panel, and it was decided that a substitute family should be found for the children. The children were placed with a white foster family. Rehabilitation was not considered, and the children remained in the care of the social services.

Black cases such as the one above occurred with such regularity that it was difficult to see them as isolated examples. The structure of social services was such that it allowed these decisions to be made in the cases of black families and children. Such decision-making occurred from the initial stage of referral through to rehabilitation.

Another factor which has to be considered in the rehabilitation and discharge of children is their legal status while in care. As already mentioned, although the majority of black children entered care via the voluntary route, they were as likely as white children to be made subject to compulsory care. In fact, black children were much more likely to be made subject to a parental rights resolution than white children.

It was found that sometimes social workers pursued the compulsory care route for no other reason than to facilitate working with parents, that is, to gain their co-operation. In the case of black families, who were perceived to be difficult to work with, this was especially relevant. Children were often made wards of court (a legal route which, was, prior to the 1989 Children Act quicker and easier than a care order) in order to ensure the compliance of parents.

In other situations, compulsory care was chosen because parents were deemed to be unfit. In the case of one black child who was voluntarily received into care because of poor housing and mother's ill-health, social services assumed rights and duties. It was argued that the mother had 'consistently failed without reasonable cause to discharge the obligations of a parent'. There appears to have been little understanding of the mother's situation.

In Chapter Five, it was shown that social workers played a very apathetic role in planning for the children's future after the initial admission into care. They had very little contact with families and children, and did little to encourage contact between parents and children. Thus children who left care had either reached the age of 18 or 19, or they were withdrawn from voluntary care by their parents. Social workers did not play an active role in these situations. Since there were only a handful of cases (including both black and white) where care orders were revoked, it could be said that those children whose legal status had become compulsory had virtually no chance of leaving care. While this applied to both black and white children, it is poignant to point out that while white children could still hope to be placed Home on Trial, black children were not so fortunate.

## Other agencies

The role played by other agencies in the referral of black families to the social services, and their influence in these situations was also examined in this study. It was found that not all black cases came to be known to the social services as a result of families referring themselves. The police and the health service were the other major referral agencies. The research showed that the police were much more likely to refer black youngsters for reasons of delinquency, while the health service was much more likely to refer cases of black mothers for reasons of mental health.

The situation of police referrals suggests that unless more black youngsters than white youngsters in the borough of Wenford were juvenile delinquents, the police as an agency were operating a system of racial discrimination. Tipler (1986) found that black youngsters were less likely to be cautioned than white youngsters and much more likely to receive custodial sentences. Evidence to support these claims has also been documented elsewhere (NACRO 1986, Taylor 1981, Walker 1988). It would appear that the black youngsters in our study were being discriminated against by the police and subsequently by the social services.

The strains and stresses of migration, and settling into a new and hostile society have been discussed elsewhere (Rack 1982). The over-representation of black people in mental institutions, particularly African-Caribbean people, is now well documented (Littlewood and Lipsedge 1982, 1989). It is increasingly being highlighted that through cultural ignorance and/or racism on the part of the psychiatric profession, black people are frequently misdiagnosed as mentally ill (Burke 1986, Cox 1986, Fernando 1988, Littlewood and Lipsedge 1989). In our study we found that quite a significant proportion of black mothers were referred by the health service for reasons of mental health. More importantly, a greater proportion of black children was admitted into care where the mother's mental health was a contributory factor than were originally referred for this reason.

The influence of other agencies/professionals upon the practices of social services in this area needs further exploration.

## Role of the black social worker

Although the employment of black social workers at a politically conscious level is a recent phenomenon, the role of such workers in the personal social services has been a point of debate since the 1960s. Many of the arguments have centred around the elusive concepts of culture and ethnicity of the clientele as well as that of the workers.

Davies (1969) recommended that the employment of more black social workers would overcome many of the difficulties. Mujahid (1971), a community relations officer, maintained that it was impossible to train a native British white social worker to deal with Asian culture. This debate which is based on the premise that cultural expertise is required to work effectively with black clients still continues today.

The borough of Wenford had made special efforts to recruit black, predominantly African-Caribbean, staff. Each area office had a significant presence of black social workers. In Areas 1, 3 and 4, black social workers constituted about a quarter of the social work staff. In Area 2, 50 per cent of the social workers were black. Such composition manifested itself in the allocation of a racially matched caseload.

Wallace, McCulloch and Kornreich (1974) argue that there is no necessary relationship between country of birth, race and culture. They assert that it is likely that because of their class position and occupational socialization, black social workers would be almost as alien to their compatriots as white, native ones. Such a criticism is also implied by Hutchinson (1969) when he states that black middle-class people and officials are westernized and hostile to their working-class compatriots. It is clear that these authors place the emphasis on knowledge of culture and the ability to empathize to the total exclusion of race and ethnicity. Also, their argument which is reduced to that of class interests lacks the more important function of social control. It is vital to recognize that whilst both black and white workers may operate to maintain hegemonic control, their effectiveness in this function is dependent upon not only their class position, but also their racial and ethnic background.

Rooney (1981) highlights the incompetent nature of equal opportunities policies by providing illustrative examples from Liverpool Social Services Department. He points to the appointment of non-white social workers who were as different from the majority of Liverpool's indigenous black population as it was possible to be in terms of ethnic and racial origins, class position, racial consciousness, and so on. While Rooney's argument is similar to that of Hutchinson (1969), and that of Wallace, McCulloch and Kornreich (1974) it is important to note that his analysis acknowledges the race dimension. That is, he not only views the differences of class and ethnicity, but also those of race.

The location of staff in the hierarchical structures of bureaucratic organizations such as social services departments is of critical significance. Black social workers in the borough of Wenford were concentrated in low grades. A great majority had working class origins. Their ability to empathize with black clients and to understand and appreciate the hostilities of a racist society was of a far superior standard than most white social workers. Although they were able to effect some positive change in the lives of black clients, workers themselves were aware of the oppressive structures which limited opportunities.

Black workers came to occupy a contradictory position in the hierarchical structure. Their ability to assess and intervene in the lives of black families, made easier by their racial and cultural background was equally matched by their ability to maintain hegemonic control over the lives of black service users. Workers felt trapped and powerless to effect any positive outcomes. It has been argued that unless social workers begin the process of understanding the many contradictions of the state, they will be nothing more than agents of the state (Bailey and Brake 1975, Corrigan and Leonard 1978, Statham 1978). Black social workers felt able to comprehend the contradictions but questioned their own ability to challenge the oppressive structures.

The enormity of the pressures within which black workers had to operate was overwhelming. Under the umbrella term 'eurocentric professional paradigm', workers expressed the constraints of their organisation, social work ideologies, education and training and social work methods. The tendency of white staff to interpret and label black workers' ways of working as 'unprofessional' was not uncommon. Black workers were accused of 'over-identification', 'emotional involvement', and of lacking the ability to maintain a 'professional distance' with their black clients. The power structures allowed such accusations to stand as professional assessments of the workers' competence.

Stubbs (1985) points out that there are real possibilities of black social workers being controlled and exploited within social services departments. Liverpool (1982) put forward the concept of the 'good black social worker', that is, one who 'colludes with the organization's view of its record in race relations'. In his study of two local authority social services departments, Stubbs quotes white social workers and managers who support their beliefs by stating that their black colleagues also think similarly. Cheetham (1981:93) discusses the exploitation from the specialist black social workers' point of view:

> Black social workers felt hopelessly isolated, misunderstood, at times snubbed and overwhelmed by totally impossible responsibilities and an unsupportive administrative structure.

It appears that black workers not only feel pressurized, but are also valued very little by their white colleagues. Stubbs (1985) found white workers to be hostile to any changes in employment practices. He argues that such hostility 'often involved a fear of an erosion of their own position or challenge to their claims to professional status and competence' (Stubbs 1985:14). The Wenford study supports the findings of Paul Stubbs. The study found that white workers perceived the employment of black workers in a wholly negative way. They felt de-skilled, resentful and professionally undermined:

> *White Social Worker*: As a social worker in an area team, whilst agreeing with positive discrimination, I think some of the appointments that have been made in the last couple of years have not been very good ones. This is my personal perspective. I think a number of people have been appointed who haven't been experienced enough to do the work, and I think this has caused a lot of friction within this particular area office. I think professional standards have dropped quite considerably in the last few years.

> *White Social Worker*: Wenford had this scheme whereby you didn't have to be qualified, you didn't have to be trained, as long as you were black.

White social workers felt that black social workers did not possess any special skills which enabled them to work more effectively with black clients. Stubbs (1985:14) quotes one social worker as saying:

> ... I've got a black student at the moment who is actually working with black kids, I don't actually believe that they've made any discernible

difference over what I and my colleagues would be doing. I don't think that these kids have shown any greater positive attitude just because the worker is black.

White social workers' professional ideologies prevented them from liaising with black colleagues for help and advice in black cases:

*Black Social Worker*: They feel that they cannot consult me because it would undermine their professionalism.

*Black Social Worker*: I don't think my colleagues can actually come to me and say, 'Look, I'm working with this black client, I've got problem x, y, z. What do you think of that?' or 'I've actually decided to do this. What do you think of that . . .'

They're (*white social workers*) not prepared to take advice from a black colleague because they think well, who the hell does she think she is? I've been here longer than she has.

In an atmosphere where white workers perceived their black colleagues to be untrained, unqualified, inexperienced, and therefore lacking in 'professionalism', it is not surprising that they failed to develop good working relations. They argued that black workers were only appointed on the basis of their 'blackness', and this was insufficient to make any significant difference to the lives of black clients. White workers' perception of the employment of black workers was a manifestation of their own fears and anxieties. Accusations of 'untrained, unqualified and inexperienced' applied more aptly to them in their dealings with black families. These white workers claimed to have an understanding of race and racism, and yet expressed desperate ignorance in their accounts of black families.

Stubbs (1985) uses the example of the black group which came into existence during his fieldwork as evidence of the fact that black social workers do make an appreciable difference which goes beyond mere ethnic sensitivity. By challenging social work values and principles, black workers were making an impact, that is, by emphasizing the importance of 'community accountability' in service provision, and by challenging the bureaucratic procedures.

While the Wenford study can confirm that black social workers do make an appreciable difference, it was found that some black workers very clearly acted as agents of the state in a highly oppressive manner to the detriment of black families and children. Their bureaucratic stance made them nothing more than mere functionaries for their department. Such workers claimed to have a special understanding of the black community networks which aided their assessment and intervention. The pressures upon these workers, as perceived by them, were not so much from the organization but from the black community:

> *Black Social Worker*: Black clients' excuses won't wash with me. I know their network, their community because I am black.

Such workers invariably began from the premise that the client was being manipulative, deceitful and making unreasonable demands. Their assessment therefore led them to employ their 'specialist knowledge' of black community networks in negative terms resulting in a poor service being offered to black clients. Although such workers were in the minority, their influence upon white colleagues and their practice cannot be underestimated. In situations where black parents argued that it did not make any appreciable difference if the worker was black or white, such workers were described as renegades. On the whole, black parents preferred black social workers. Although they felt able to relate to them better, these parents felt that they could not ask for a black worker because it might be construed as racist.

While the collective action of black social workers in some local authorities has proved to be influential in shaping policy and provision, it has to be borne in mind that, on the whole, the contribution of black workers has only been incremental. This is largely due to their position in the power structure. In his analysis of Lambeth Council, Ousley (1982) states that there was an under-representation of black workers within the directorate. The disparity was particularly pronounced amongst 'senior management' with black staff occupying only 4 per cent in total and none of the 53 most senior posts, and 'specialist, professional and practitioner' posts. Overall, some 80 per cent of the total black staff in the directorate was concentrated in the lowest three, non-social work, grades. A not too dissimilar picture was found in the borough of Wenford.

The role played by black workers is highly constrained and difficult. The majority of black social workers operate in the face of oppression and discrimination in attempting to provide an effective service to clients. They strive to use their background and position of power for positive benefit to clients. Despite the unsupportive environment, and feelings of powerlessness, these workers do make an appreciable impact in their work. They are able to form better relationships with their clients because they are able to empathize with their situation. In this study, such workers were able to engage black families in preventative strategies to obviate the admission of black children into care. Moreover, they were able to foster better links between parents and children and thus pursue programmes of rehabilitation and discharge. However, their role was limited in the face of institutional and cultural racism embedded in bureaucratic structures and policies which negated the possibility of achieving effective change in the lives of black families and children.

## Summary and conclusion

It is evident that black and white children experience a different reality in the care system. The differences exist not only at the stage of referral and admission, but continue throughout the care career process. An understanding of the socio-economic situation of black families is insufficient to understand this phenomenon. Factors such as the organization of social work and its lack of relevance to the needs of black communities, social work ideologies, education and training, and social work methods need to be conceptualized in the context of the ways in which cases of black families are processed in the personal social services. It is argued that the oppressive structures of the organization, coupled with eurocentric policies, social work theory and practice, and professional ideologies result in a situation where black families and children receive a qualitatively poor service. Constructions of the black family as deficient, incomplete, repressive and deviant are reproduced in social work ideology, theory and practice and manifested in the institutional processes. As a consequence of such constraints, black and white workers come to occupy a contradictory position which they must challenge to provide an adequate service to families and children.

# 7

# *Conclusions*

The findings of this study concerning the care careers of black children are both encouraging and bleak. The encouraging findings include the placement of black children in racially and culturally appropriate family settings, regular contact between black children in care and their families, and the efforts of residential settings to move away from the eurocentric framework to anti-racist ways of working. The employment of black workers, in more than just a tokenistic way, is clearly a step in the right direction. It is also useful to learn that for the majority of black children, route of entry into care is voluntary. The need for preventative strategies in the early stages of the referral is therefore crucial and needs careful consideration.

It is troubling to note that black children are severely dispropor-tionately represented in care, enter care twice as quickly as white children, and are as likely as white children to be made subject to compulsory care even where the initial admission was voluntary. There was less preventive work done with black families. While greater efforts were made not to admit white children into care, the same was not true for black children. Social workers' negative perceptions of black families led them to develop a 'rescue mentality' which came into force very quickly when dealing with these families. Social workers' image of black parents as 'hostile and uncooperative' prevented them from working effectively with black families. This played a part not only at the initial stage of admission but was very much in operation in the later stages. Also disheartening is the finding that some minority ethnic children's placement and identity needs were not being adequately met. The inappropriate placement of West African, Asian and Turkish Cypriot children is the manifestation of social services' ignorance of cultural and ethnic complexities. It is disturbing to note that despite the good parental links, black children had only a slim chance of being placed Home on Trial. Social workers' inability to engage black families in the early stages of referral suggests devastating consequences for subsequent child care careers.

## Implications of findings in the context of 1989 Children Act

This study was conducted two years before the new child care legislation was passed, which for the first time in the history of British child care legislation incorporated race and ethnicity as elements of consideration. Although concepts such as race, culture, language and religion have only been put forward as issues of consideration for the local authorities, the 1989 Children Act is nevertheless a vehicle for the promotion of good practice with black and white families. The key principle of partnership is at the crux of the matter, and one which social services need to espouse wholeheartedly.

Partnership with families is an equal opportunities exercise, and incorporates concepts of co-working, agreement, collaboration, and contracts. If these are to be translated into action, social workers and social services departments as organizations need to accept the challenges presented by the 1989 Children Act. This study supports the findings of previous mainstream studies in highlighting the lack of partnership between social services and families Vernon and Fruin 1986, Millham 1986). In the absence of partnership, an atmosphere of distrust will result in families being reluctant to come forward, hindering possibilities of collective working.

There are several areas in which the 1989 Children Act can make an appreciable difference to black child care careers. In relation to the findings of this study, four aspects are identified below. Firstly, in the initial stage of admission into care, social services need to improve their practices to conduct assessments which take cognisance of the pervading effects of race and racism upon the lives of black service users. An understanding of cultural complexities is crucial but should not be perceived as mutually exclusive to the concepts of race and racism. The two are intertwined and need to be embraced in a similar vein. Working in partnership with black families needs to be against a backcloth of such a framework where issues of culture, ethnicity, and race and racism are carefully and appropriately balanced.

State social work tends to perpetuate oppressive social relations by its ability to impose its own definition of the 'good family' as two

121

parents, white, middle class, heterosexual and able-bodied. To enhance the dignity and respect of individuals and families, social workers need to develop a self awareness of race, class, gender, sexual orientation and disability.

Effectiveness research shows that commonly agreed problems/goals lead to more productive and effective outcomes (Wilson 1985, Olin 1986). Social workers' ability to conduct appropriate assessments and engage black families to move towards commonly agreed goals will make a marked difference to black child care careers. Two findings of this study which show that black children are more likely to enter voluntary care and are admitted into care twice as quickly as white children, are indictments of the system which claims to take preventative measures to obviate admission of children into care. Social services need to take up the professional opportunity and challenge to develop ways which will reduce the need for black children to be accommodated under the 1989 Children Act.

Secondly, with regard to the placement of children in racially and culturally appropriate settings, the borough of Wenford had made huge strides. The efforts of the department in this area of work should be highly commended. One source of concern, however, was the marginalization of some minority ethnic children. Their inappropriate placement contravened the department's otherwise progressive stance on same race placements. A great deal of work needs to be done in this area if the meaning of the new child care legislation is to become reality for all groups concerned. Recruitment of minority ethnic foster carers should be an important priority. Also, the ethos of residential homes which may still be eurocentric needs careful consideration. Particular attention should be paid to the employment of black residential social workers and the cultural, linguistic, religious and health and dietry needs of black children. Working strategies should be developed which take account of the experiences of black children. The establishment of therapeutic units to address the emotional and psychological needs of all black children, but particularly those with negative experiences of transracial settings, is essential.

Thirdly, in the area of rehabilitation and discharge, recognition needs to be made of the problems being experienced by parents, and how social services can assist to improve their situation. William Ackroyd, the foster carers' solicitor in the Jasmine Beckford inquiry, argued that social workers were worried about being called racist if they did not rehabilitate Jasmine back with her parents (Hencke 1986). Arguments such as these, taken out of context as they invariable are, serve to do grave injustice to black families and social workers engaged in the anti-racist struggle.

Social services need to continue working in partnership at the stage when the child is in care, and facilitate better links between black families and children. Sibling contact should be maintained and social workers need to be actively involved in promoting peer group contact, due to its importance for social development and identity.

Finally, social services need to be able to deal with people at the level they present themselves, and participation in decision making is vital. The giving and receiving of information is crucial to encourage the smooth turning of the wheels of a child's care career. The concept of empowerment has been much bandied about but needs to be recognized as a force for action and activity to avoid it becoming a mere lip service tool. Corporate negotiations, advocacy, and arbitration are important mechanisms in the development of empowerment as a tool for action. The importance of cultural relativism, issues of race and racism need to be given consideration to develop strategies of empowerment with all client groups.

The Wenford findings point to a lamentable failure on the part of the social services to develop appropriate and adequate service and improve practice and policy. The study underlies and supports the requirements in the 1989 Children Act.

Black people live in an extremely race conscious society which militates powerful pressures upon them. It is essential for social workers to understand their internal and external reality. Thus, the political, economic, societal and historical frameworks, as well as individual dynamics, must be appreciated if the difficulties of black people are not to be marginalized.

This research has established some of the similarities and differences between black and white child care careers. It was found that black families and children underwent a qualitatively different and inferior experience in their dealings with the social services. An examination of social work policy, theory and practice, and provision has illustrated the processes which lead to differential treatment. It is hoped that the study will not only contribute to our understanding of child care careers of black children, but will also facilitate a more socially reflective stance to the pragmatic and policy issues of state social work.

# *APPENDIX*

Supplementary figures and tables referred to in the text.

*Figure 3.5   Change in legal status by race (%)*

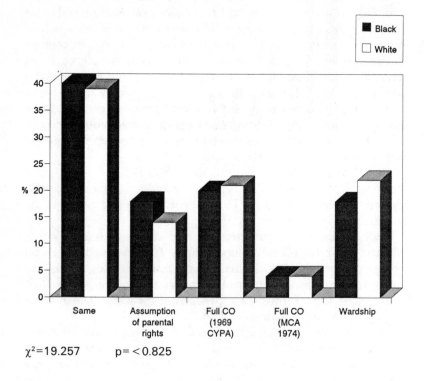

$\chi^2 = 19.257$        $p = <0.825$

*Figure 4.2   Placement at time of study by race (%)*

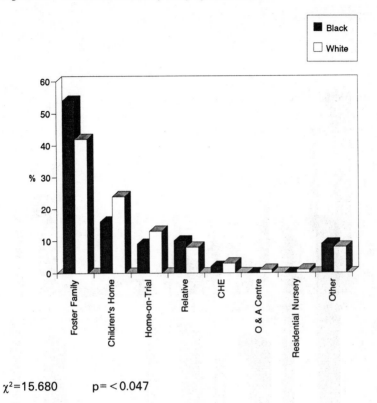

$\chi^2 = 15.680$        $p = < 0.047$

*Figure 4.3   Placement upon follow-up by race (%)*

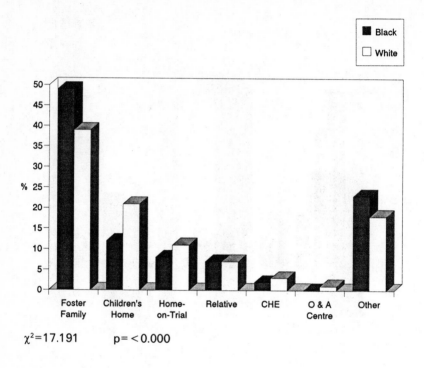

$\chi^2 = 17.191$        $p = < 0.000$

*Figure 5.2   Parental links upon follow-up by race (%)*

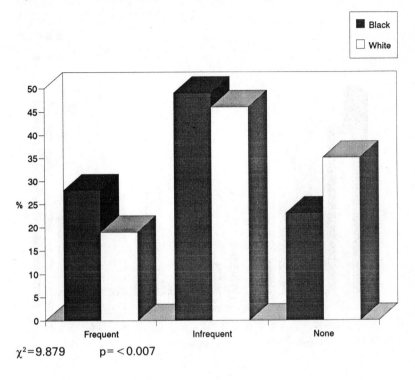

$\chi^2 = 9.879$         $p = < 0.007$

*Figure 5.3   Parental links of children placed in foster families by child's race (%)*

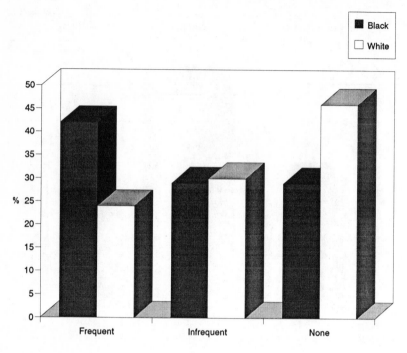

*Table 3.3   Admissions into care by race by year, 1983–1986 (%)*

| Year | Black | White | Total |
|------|-------|-------|-------|
| 1983 | 61 | 39 | 100 (49) |
| 1984 | 51 | 49 | 100 (47) |
| 1985 | 51 | 49 | 100 (81) |
| 1986 | 56 | 44 | 100 (94) |

*Table 4.1   Total number of placements (related to all care episodes) by race (%)*

| No. of placements | Black | White |
|---|---|---|
| 1–2 | 35 | 38 |
| 3–5 | 38 | 35 |
| 6 or more | 27 | 27 |
| Total (%) (n) | 100 (294) | 100 (270) |

*Table 5.1   Parental links of children placed in Children's Homes by race (%)*

| Parental links | Black % | Black (n) | White % | White (n) |
|---|---|---|---|---|
| Frequent | 42 | (20) | 46 | (29) |
| Infrequent | 44 | (21) | 43 | (27) |
| None | 14 | (7) | 11 | (7) |
| Total | 100 | (48) | 100 | (63) |

*Table 5.2   Parental links of children placed with relatives by race (%)*

| Parental links | Black % | Black (n) | White % | White (n) |
|---|---|---|---|---|
| Frequent | 63 | (15) | 50 | (10) |
| Infrequent | 21 | (5) | 20 | (4) |
| None | 16 | (4) | 30 | (6) |
| Total | 100 | (24) | 100 | (20) |

*Table 5.3   Social worker contact with natural family by child's race (%)*

| SW Contact | Black | White | All |
|---|---|---|---|
| Frequent | 8 | 7 | 7 |
| Infrequent | 52 | 51 | 52 |
| None | 40 | 42 | 41 |
| Total (%)<br>(n) | 100<br>(280) | 100<br>(264) | 100<br>(544) |

*Table 5.4   Home on Trial by race by area (%)*

| Area Office | Black | White | Total | (n) |
|---|---|---|---|---|
| Area 1 | 41 | 37 | 39 | (35) |
| Area 2 | 19 | 35 | 26 | (45) |
| Area 3 | 25 | 37 | 30 | (52) |
| Area 4 | 6 | 23 | 15 | (19) |
| Borough | 21 | 33 | 27 | (151) |

*Table 5.5   Children in/out of care upon follow-up by race (%)*

| In/out of care | Black | White | All |
|---|---|---|---|
| In care | 83 | 87 | 85 |
| Out of care | 17 | 13 | 15 |
| Total (%)<br>(n) | 100<br>(288) | 100<br>(270) | 100<br>(558) |

$\chi^2 = 2.44$ p = < 0.294

Table 5.6 *Length of time between admission and discharge by race (%)*

| Length of time | Black | White |
|---|---|---|
| Less than a year | 23 | 22 |
| 1–2 years | 19 | 3 |
| Over 2 years | 58 | 75 |
| Total (%)<br>(n) | 100<br>(43) | 100<br>(32) |

# Bibliography

ABEL-SMITH, B. and TOWNSEND, P. 'The Poor and the Poorest', Occasional Paper on Social Administration, no 17, Bell and Sons, 1965

ADAMS, R.N. and PRIESS, J.J. (eds) *Human Organisation Research, Field Relations and Techniques*, Dorsey Press, 1960

ADCOCK, M, WHITE, R. and ROWLANDS, O. *The Administrative Parent – A study of the assumptions of parental rights and duties*, British Agencies for Adoption and Fostering, 1983

AHMAD, B. *Black Perspectives in Social Work*, Venture Press, 1990

AHMAD, B. 'The Development of Social Work Practice and Policies on Race', *Social Work Today*, 14 January 1988

AHMED, S. 'Asian Girls and Culture Conflict' in CHEETHAM, J. et al, (eds) *Social and Community Work in a Multi-Racial Society*, Harper & Row, 1981

AHMED, S. 'Children in Care. The Racial Dimension in Social Work Assessment' in CHEETHAM, J. et al (eds) *Social and Community Work in a Multi-Racial Society*, Harper & Row, 1981

AHMED, S, CHEETHAM, J. and SMALL, J. (eds) *Social Work with Black Families and Children*, Batsford, 1986

ALLEN, S. 'The Institutionalisation of Racism', *Race*, 15(1), 1973

ALTHUSSER, L. *For Marx*, Penguin, 1969

ARNOLD, E. 'Finding Black Families for Black Children in Britain' in CHEETHAM, J. (ed) *Social Work and Ethnicity*, Allen & Unwin, 1982

ASSOCIATION OF BLACK SOCIAL WORKERS AND ALLIED PROFESSIONS, *Black Children in Care: Evidence to the House of Commons Social Services Committee*, ABSWAP, 1983

ASSOCIATION OF DIRECTORS OF SOCIAL SERVICES 'Social Services and Ethnic Minorities, Report of a Questionnaire Survey on Social Services Departments and Ethnic Minorities', ADSS, 1983

AYMER, C. 'Women in Residential Work: Dilemmas and Ambiguities', in LANGAN, M. and DAY, L. (eds), *Women, Oppression and Social Work, Issues in Anti-Discriminatory Practice*, Routledge, 1992

BAGLEY, C. and YOUNG, L. 'Policy Dilemmas and the Adoption of Black Children' in CHEETHAM, J. (ed) *Social Work and Ethnicity*, Allen & Unwin, 1982

BAILEY, R. and BRAKE, M. (eds) *Radical Social Work*, Edward Arnold, 1975

BALLARD, R. 'Ethnic Minorities and the Social Services: What Type of service?' in KHAN, V. (ed) *Minority Families in Britain*, Macmillan, 1979

BANKS, N. (1992) 'Techniques for direct identity work with black children', *Adoption and Fostering*, 16(3), 19–25.

BARN, R. 'Black children in local authority care: admission patterns', *New Community*, 16(2), 1990, pp. 229–46

BARN, R. 'Anti-Discriminatory Research in Social Work: Some issues for consideration: Social Research Association Newsletter, 1992.

BARNARDO'S 'Racial Integration and Barnardo's: Report of a Working Party', Barnardo's, 1966

BATTA, I, McCULLOCH, J. and SMITH, N. 'A Study of Juvenile Delinquency amongst Asians and Half-Asians', *British Journal of Criminology*, 15(1), 1975, pp. 32–42

BATTA, I. and MAWBY, R. 'Children in Local Authority Care: A Monitoring of Racial Differences in Bradford', *Policy And Politics*, 9(2), 1981, pp. 137–49

BATTA, I, MAWBY, R. and McCULLOCH, J. 'Crime, Social Problems and Asian Immigration: The Bradford Experience', *International Journal of Contemporary Sociology*, 18(1), 1981, pp. 135–68

BEBBINGTON, A.C. and MILES, J.B. 'Children's GRE Research: Children Entering Care, A need indicator for in-care services for children', Discussion Paper No. 574/A, Personal Social Services Research Unit, University of Kent, 1988

BEBBINGTON, A and MILES, J. 'The Background of Children who enter Local Authority Care', British Journal of Social Work, 19(5), 1989

BELL, C. and NEWBY, H. *Doing Sociological Research*, Allen & Unwin, 1977

BELL, C. and ENCEL, S. (eds) *Inside the Whale: Ten Personal Accounts of Social Research*, Pergamon, 1978

BEN-TOVIM, G. and GABRIEL, S. 'The politics of race in Britain, 1962–79: a review of the major trends and of recent debates', in HUSBAND, C. (ed) *'Race' in Britain, Continuity and Change*, Hutchinson, 1982

BERRIDGE, D. *Children's Homes*, Blackwell, 1985

BERRY, J. *Social Work with Children*, Routledge and Kegan Paul, 1972

BHAT, A; CARR-HILL, R, and OHRI, S. *Britain's Black Population: A New Perspective*, 2nd edition, Gower, 1988

BLACK AND IN CARE *Black and in Care: Conference Report*, Blackrose Press, 1984

BLAXTER, M. and PATTERSON, E. *Mothers and Daughters*, Heinemann, 1982

BLUMER, H. 'What is wrong with Social Theory', *American Sociological Review*, 19(1), 1954

BOGGS, C. *Gramsci's Marxism*, Pluto Press, 1976

BOSS, P. and HOMESHAW, J. 'Britain's Black Citizens: A Comparative Study of Social Work with Coloured Families and their White Indigenous Neighbours', *Social Work Today*, 6(12), 1975

BOSS, P. and HOMESHAW, J. 'Coloured Families and Social Services Departments', Research Report, University of Leicester, School of Social Work, 1974

BOURNE, J. 'Cheerleaders and Ombudsmen: the Sociology of Race Relations in Britain', *Race and Class*, 20(4), 1980

BREWER, C. and LAIT, J. *Can Social Work Survive?* Temple Smith, 1980

BRITISH ASSOCIATION OF SOCIAL WORKERS 'Social Work Practice with

Children and Families Advisory Panel, The Assumption of Parental Rights and Duties', BASW, 1982

BRITISH ASSOCIATION OF SOCIAL WORKERS 'Evidence to the House of Commons Social Services Committee Inquiry into Children in Care', BASW, 1983

BRITISH ASSOCIATION OF SOCIAL WORKERS 'Response to the Second Report from the Social Services Committee (Session 1983–84) on Children in Care', BASW, 1984

BRITISH ASSOCIATION OF SOCIAL WORKERS 'Report to the Project Group Established by the Professional Practice Divisional Committee to Respond to the Inter-Departmental Working Party on Child Care Law', BASW, 1985

BRITISH ASSOCIATION OF SOCIAL WORKERS 'Social Work and Racism Group, Birmingham and Solihull BASW Branch, Conference Notes', BASW, 1987

BROWN, C. *Black and White Britain*, HEB/Policy Studies Institute, 1984

BROWN, J.S. and GILMARTIN, B.G. 'Sociology Today: Lacunae, Emphasis and Surfeiting', *American Sociologist 4*, 1969, pp. 283–291

BRUMMER, N. 'White Social Worker/Black Children: Issues of Identity', in ALDGATE J. and SIMMONDS J. (eds), *Direct Work with Children, A Guide for Social Work Practitioners*, Batsford, 1988

BRYAN, A. 'Working with Black Single Mothers: Myths and Reality', in LANGAN M. and DAY L. (eds), *Women, Oppression and Social Work, Issues in Anti-Discriminatory Practice*, Routledge, 1992

BUCI-GLUCKMAN, C. *Gramsci and the State*, Lawrence and Wishart, 1980

BULMER, M. *Sociological Research Methods*, Macmillan, 1984

BURGESS, B. *Key Variables in Social Research*, Routledge and Kegan Paul, 1986

BURGESS, B. *In the Field*, Allen & Unwin, 1984

BURGESS, B. (ed) *Field Research, A Sourcebook and Field Manual*, Allen & Unwin, 1982

BURGESS, B. (ed) *Studies in Qualitative Methodology*, Vol.1, Jai Press, 1988

BURGESS, C. *In Care and into Work*, Tavistock, 1981

BURKE, A. 'Racism, Prejudice and Mental Illness', in Cox, J. (ed) *Transcultural Psychiatry*, Croom Helm, 1986

BYNNER, J. and STRIBLEY, M. (eds) *Social Research: Principles and Procedures*, Open University Press, 1985

CAMPAIGN AGAINST RACISM AND FASCISM (CARF) 'Racism and Children in Care', *Race and Class*, 35(2), 1983

CARBY, H. 'Schooling in Babylon', in CCCS, *The Empire Strikes Back, Race and Racism in 70s Britain*, Hutchinson, 1982

CARMICHAEL, S. and HAMILTON, C.V. *Black Power: The Politics of Liberation in America*, Jonathan Cape, 1968

CAWSON, P. *Black Children in Approved Schools*, Department of Health and Social Security, 1977

CENTRAL COUNCIL FOR EDUCATION AND TRAINING IN SOCIAL WORK, (CCETSW), *Setting the Context for Change, Anti-Racist Social Work Education*, CCETSW, 1991

CENTRAL STATISTICAL OFFICE 'Percentage of Husbands and Wives Married to White Persons: by Ethnic Group and Age', *Social Trends*, vol 18, HMSO, 1988

CENTRE FOR CONTEMPORARY CULTURAL STUDIES, (CCCS) *The Empire Strikes Back, Race and Racism in 70s Britain*, Hutchinson, 1982

CHALLIS, L. 'Review and Consolidation in Brent Social Services', Centre for the Analysis of Social Policy, University of Bath, 1987

CHEETHAM, J. *Social Work with Immigrants*, Routledge and Kegan Paul, 1972

CHEETHAM, J. 'Social Work Services for Ethnic Minorities in Britain and the USA', Department of Health and Social Security, 1981

CHEETHAM, J. 'Positive Discrimination in Social Work: Negotiating the Opposition', *New Community*, 10(1), 1982

CHEETHAM, J. (ed) *Social Work and Ethnicity*, Allen & Unwin, 1982

CHEETHAM, J. (ed) *Social and Community Work in a Multi-Racial Society*, Harper & Row, 1981

CHEETHAM, J. 'Values in Action', in SHARDLOW, S. (ed) *The Values of Change in Social Work*, Tavistock/Routledge, 1989

CLARE WENGER, G. (ed) *The Research Relationship, Practice and Policy in Social Policy Research*, Allen & Unwin, 1987

CLARKE, C.L. and ASQUITH, S. *Social Work and Social Philosophy, A Guide for Practice*, Routledge and Kegan Paul, 1985

CLEGG, S. *The Theory of Power and Organisations*, Routledge and Kegan Paul, 1979

COFFIELD, F, ROBINSON, J. and SARSBY, J. *A Cycle of Deprivation? A Case Study of Four Families*, Heinemann, 1982

COMMISSION FOR RACIAL EQUALITY 'A Home from Home? Some Policy Considerations on Black Children in Residential Care', CRE, 1977

COMMISSION FOR RACIAL EQUALITY/ASSOCIATION OF DIRECTORS OF SOCIAL SERVICES 'Multi-Racial Britain: The Social Services Response', CRE/ADSS, 1978

COMMISSION FOR RACIAL EQUALITY, EEC LABOUR FORCE SURVEY 'Ethnic Minorities in Britain: Statistical Information on the Pattern of Settlement', CRE, 1981

COMMISSION FOR RACIAL EQUALITY 'Immigration Control Procedures: Report of a Formal Investigation', CRE, 1985

COMMISSION FOR RACIAL EQUALITY 'Race Equality in Social Services Departments, A Survey of Opportunity Policies', CRE, 1989

CONNELLY, N. *Social Services Provision in Multi-Racial Areas*, Policy Studies Institute, 1981

CONNELLY, N. 'Social Services Departments and Race: A Discussion Paper', Discussion Paper No. 12, Policy Studies Institute, 1985

COOPERSMITH, S. *The Antecedents of Self-Esteem*, Freeman, 1967

CORRIGAN, P. and LEONARD, P. *Social Work Practice under Capitalism: A Marxist Approach*, Macmillan, 1978

COULSHED, V. *Social Work Practice, An Introduction*, 2nd edn, Macmillan, 1992

COX, J. *Transcultural Psychiatry*, Croom Helm, 1986

DALE, A; ARBER, S. and PROCTER, M. *Doing Secondary Analysis*, Allen & Unwin, 1988

DALE, D. 'Denying Homes to Black Children: Britain's New Race Policies', Social Affairs Unit, Research Report 8, 1987

DANIEL, W.W. *Racial Discrimination in England*, Penguin, 1968

DAVIES, J.W.D. 'Immigrants – part two – in Britain', *Child Care*, 23, 55, 1969

DAY, D. *The Adoption of Black Children*, D.C. Heath, 1977

DE LA MOTTA, C. 'Blacks in the Criminal Justice System', Unpublished MSc thesis, University of Aston, 1984

DEAKIN, N. 'Inner Areas: An Ethnic Dimension?', Discussion Paper to CES Workshop, 1978

DEPARTMENT OF THE ENVIRONMENT 'Policy for Inner Cities', Cmnd 6845, DOE, HMSO, 1977

DEPARTMENT OF HEALTH AND SOCIAL SECURITY 'Children in Care of Local Authorities, Year ending 31st March 1983', England, A/F 83/12, DHSS, 1983

DEPARTMENT OF HEALTH AND SOCIAL SECURITY, 'Children in Care, Government Response To The Second Report From The Social Services Committee, Session 1983–84, HMSO

DEPARTMENT OF HEALTH AND SOCIAL SECURITY, 'Code of Practice, Access to Children in Care, Laid before Parliament on 16th December 1983 pursuant to section 12G (3) of the Child Care Act 1980', HMSO

DEPARTMENT OF HEALTH AND SOCIAL SECURITY 'Social Work Decisions in Child Care: Recent Research Findings and their Implications', HMSO, 1985

DINGWALL, R., EEKELAAR, J. and MURRAY, T. *The Protection of Children: State Intervention and Family Life*, Basil Blackwell, 1983

DIVINE, D. 'Defective, Hypocritical and Patronising Research', *Caribbean Times*, 4 March 1983

DIVINE, D. 'No Problems', Article on Gill and Jackson's Research Study, *Caribbean Times*, Feb/March 1983

DIVINE, D. 'Submission to the Jasmine Beckford Inquiry Report', June 1985

DOMINELLI, L. 'Anti-Racist Social Work', Macmillan/British Association of Social Workers, 1988

DUFFIELD, M. *Social Work Today*, April 1985

DUMMETT, A. *A Portrait of English Racism*, Penguin, 1973

DUMMETT, A. *Citizenship and Nationality*, Runnymede Trust, 1976

EDWARD, J. and BATLEY, R. *The Politics of Positive Discrimination in England*, Tavistock, 1978

ELLIS, J. (ed) *West African Families in Britain*, Routledge and Kegan Paul, 1978

ELY, P. and DENNEY, D. *Social Work in a Multi-Racial Society*, Gower, 1987

ENGELS, F. *The Condition of the Working Class in England*, Blackwell, 1971

ERIKSON, E. *Identity, Youth and Crisis*, Faber & Faber, 1968

FANSHEL, D. *Far from the Reservation: The Transracial Adoption of American Indian Children*, Scarecrow Press, 1972

FARMER, E. and PARKER, R. *A Study of Interim Care Orders*, School of Applied Social Studies, University of Bristol, 1985

FERNANDO, S. *Race and Culture in Psychiatry*, Croom Helm, 1988

FIFTH REPORT FROM THE HOME AFFAIRS COMMITTEE, Session 1980–1981, Racial Disadvantage, 1, HC 424-I, 1981

FIRST KEY *A Study of Black Young People Leaving Care*, CRE, 1987

FISHER, M, MARSH, P, PHILLIPS, D. and SAINSBURY, E. *In and Out of Care*, Batsford/British Agencies for Adoption and Fostering, 1986

FITZHERBERT, K. *West Indian Children In London*, Bell and Sons, 1967

FITZGERALD, M. *Political Parties and Black People*, Runnymede Trust, 1984

FOREN, R. and BATTA, I. '"Colour" as a variable in the use made of a Local Authority Child Care Department', *Social Work*, 27(3), 1970, pp. 10–15

GABRIEL, S.C. 'The Colonial Legacy and its Impact on Black Psychology in the Western World', Unpublished, Inner-City Mental Health Team, Bristol, 1989

GALE, J.A.B. 'Non-European Children in Care', *Child Care Quarterly Review*, 17(4), 1963

GARCIA, A. 'Cultural Desensitisation: The Effects of the Bleaching Process in Social Work Education', Conference paper given at CCETSW organized conference, 14/15 November 1990, Black Perspectives in Social Work Education

GARNETT, L. *Leaving Care and After*, NCB, 1992

GEORGE, V. and WILDING, P. *Ideology and Social Welfare*, Routledge and Kegan Paul, 1985

GILL, O. and JACKSON, B. *Adoption and Race*, Batsford, 1983

GILROY, P. *There ain't no Black in the Union Jack*, Hutchinson, 1987

GOFFMAN, E. *Asylums: Essays on the Social Situation of Mental Patients and Other Inmates*, Penguin, 1961

GOULDNER, A.W. *Patterns of Industrial Bureaucracy*, Glencoe, III: The Free Press, 1954

GREER, S. *The Logic of Social Inquiry*, Aldine Publishing Company, 1969

GROW, L.C. and SHAPIRO, D. *Black Children, White Parents: A Study of Transracial Adoption*, Child Welfare League of America, 1974

'Plea to Mellor in Mixed Race Adoption Row', The *Guardian*, 25 August 1989

HADLEY, R. and HATCH, S. *Social Welfare and the Failure of the State*, Allen & Unwin, 1981

HAKIM, C. *Research Design: Strategies and Choices in the Design of Social Research*, Allen & Unwin, 1987

HALL, S. 'Racism and Reaction', in *Commission for Racial Equality, Five Views of Multi-Racial Britain*, BBC/CRE, 1978

HALL, S. et al *Policing the Crisis: Mugging, the State, and Law and Order*, Macmillan, 1978

HALL, S. *Gramsci's Relevance to the Analysis of Racism and Ethnicity*, for UNESCO, Division of Human Rights and Peace, 1984

HALL, T. 'Submission to the Jasmine Beckford Inquiry Report', British Association for Adoption and Fostering, 1985

HEMSLEY, J. 'Stepping out into unknown territory', *Community Care*, 21 November 1985

HENCKE, D. 'Jasmine case team "feared racism claim"', The *Guardian*, 12 March 1986

HEPTINSTALL, D. 'The Black Perspective', *Community Care*, 31 July 1986

HILDREW, P. 'Children "being needlessly taken into care"', The *Guardian*, 18 September 1986

HILGENDORF, L. *Social Workers and Solicitors in Child Care Cases*, HMSO, 1981

HIRO, D. *Black British, White British*, Eyre and Spottiswoode, 1971

HOARE, Q. and NOWELL SMITH, G. *Selections from the Prison Notebooks of Antonio Gramsci*, London: Lawrence and Wishart, 1971

HOLMAN, R. 'The foster child and self-knowledge', Case Conference, 12, 1966, pp. 295–98

HOLMAN, R. *Putting Children First*, Macmillan, 1988

HOME OFFICE *Racial Discrimination*, Cmnd 6234, HMSO, 1975

HOUSE OF COMMONS SOCIAL SERVICES COMMITTEE *Children In Care*, HMSO, 1984

HOWE, D. *Social Workers and their Practice in Welfare Bureaucracies*, Gower, 1986

HUSBAND, C. 'Notes on Racism in Social Work Practice', *Multi-Racial Social Work*, 1, 1980, pp. 5–15

HUSBAND, C. (ed) *'Race' in Britain, Continuity and Change*, Hutchinson, 1982

HUTCHINSON, P. 'The social worker and culture conflict', Case Conference, 15, 467, 1969

HYNDMAN, A. The Welfare of Coloured People in London, *Social Work*, 15, 1958

INGLEBY COMMITTEE *The Child, the Family and the Young Offender*, HMSO, 1965

IRWINE, J. et al *Demystifying Social Statistics*, Pluto, 1979

JACKSON, B. *Family Experiences of Inter-Racial Adoption*, Association of British Adoption Agencies, 1976

JACKSON, S. *The Education of Children in Care*, Paper for Economic and Social Research Council, 1983

JANSARI, A. 'Social Work with Ethnic Minorities: A Review of the Literature', *Multi-Racial Social Work*, 1, 1980, pp. 17–34

JASMINE BECKFORD INQUIRY REPORT Brent Borough Council, A Child In Trust, 1985

JENKINS, S. *The Ethnic Dilemma in Social Services*, The Free Press, 1981

JOHNSON, M.R.D. and CROSS, M. 'Surveying Service Users', Research Paper 2, University of Warwick, Centre for Research in Ethnic Relations, 1984

JOHNSON, M.R.D. 'Citizenship, Social Work and Ethnic Minorities', in ETHERINGTON S. (ed) *Social Work and Citizenship*, British Association of Social Workers, 1986

JOHNSON, T.J. *Professions and Power*, Macmillan, 1972

JOLL, J. *Gramsci*, Fontana/Collins, 1977

JONES, C. *State Social Work and the Working Class*, Routledge and Kegan Paul, 1983

KARENGA, M. *Introduction to Black Studies*, Kawaida Publications, Los Angeles, 1982

KAUR, R. 'The Race Dilemma in the Personal Social Services: A Case Study of Wolverhampton', Dissertation Submitted for the B.A (Hons) Sociology, City of Birmingham Polytechnic, 1985

KENT, B. 'The Social Worker's Cultural Pattern as it Affects Casework with Immigrants', in TRISELIOTIS, J.P. (ed) *Social Work with Coloured Immigrants and their Families*, Oxford University Press, 1972

KAHN, R.L. and CANNELL, C.F. *The Dynamics of Interviewing, Theory, Technique and Cases*, Wiley and Sons, 1957

KHAN, V.S. *Minority Families in Britain: Support and Stress*, Macmillan, 1979

KOH, F.M. *Oriental Children in American Homes: How do they adjust?* East West Press, 1988

KORNREICH, R. et al 'Social Workers' Attitudes Towards Immigrant Clients', A Summary of the Research Project, School of Applied Social Studies, University of Bradford, 1973

KNIGHT, L. 'Giving Her Roots', *Community Care*, 166, 1977

LOCAL GOVERNMENT MANAGEMENT BOARD *The Unequal Challenge*, LGMB, 1991

LABOV, W. *Language in the Inner-City, Studies in the Black English Vernacular*, Blackwell, 1977

LADNER, J. *Mixed-Families: Adoption Across Racial Boundaries*, Anchor Press/Doubleday, 1977

LAMBETH DIRECTORATE OF SOCIAL SERVICES 'Black Children in Care', Research Section, Lambeth, N. Adams, 1981

LAMBERT, J. *Crime, Police and Race Relations*, Oxford University Press, 1970

LANGAN, M and DAY, L. (eds) *Women, Oppression and Social Work, Issues in Anti-Discriminatory Practice*, Routledge, 1992

LAURANCE, J. 'White children placed in black foster homes', *Observer*, 17 May 1987

LAWRENCE, E. 'Common Sense, Racism and the Sociology of Race Relations', Centre for Contemporary Cultural studies, Stencilled Occasional Paper, no.66, 1981

LESTOR, J. 'Putting the Children First', *The Voice*, 5 July 1986

LINDSAY-SMITH, C. *Black Children in Care: A Summary Report of a Feasibility Study undertaken for the Association of British Adoption and Fostering Agencies and the Runnymede Trust*, Allen & Unwin, 1979

LIPSKY, M. *Street Level Bureaucracy*, Russell Sage Foundation, 1980

LITTLEWOOD, R. and LIPSEDGE, M. *Aliens and Alienists*, Penguin, 1982

LITTLEWOOD, R. and LIPSEDGE, M. *Aliens and Alienists*, Unwin Hyman, 1989

LIVERPOOL, V. 'The Dilemmas and Contributions of Black Social Workers', in CHEETHAM, J. (ed) *Social Work and Ethnicity*, Allen & Unwin, 1982

LIVERPOOL, V. 'When Backgrounds Clash', *Community Care*, 2 October 1986: pp. 19–21

LONDON BOROUGH OF LAMBETH 'Whose Child? The report of the panel appointed to inquire into the death of Tyra Henry', London Borough of Lambeth, 1987

McADOO, H.P. (ed) *Black Families*, Sage Publications, 1988

McCulloch, J, Batta, I. and Smith, N. 'Colour as a variable in the Childrens' Section of a Local Authority Social Services Department', *New Community*, 7, 1979, pp. 78–84

McCulloch, J.W. and Kornreich, R. 'Black People and the Social Services Departments, Problems and Perspectives', in Brown M.J. (ed) *Social Issues in the Social Services*, Charles Knight, 1974

McCulloch, J. and Smith, N. 'Blacks and Social Work', *New Society*, 25 April 1974

Magee, B. *Popper*, Fontana, 1973

Manchester Law Centre *But My Cows aren't Going to England*, 1986

Marsland, D. *Sociological Explorations in the Service of Youth*, National Youth Bureau, 1978

Mayer, J.G. and Timms, N. *The Client Speaks, Working-Class Impressions of Casework*, Routledge and Kegan Paul, 1970

Mays, J, Forder, A. and *Keidan, O. Penelope Hall's Social Services of England and Wales*, Routledge and Kegan Paul, 1983

Merton, R. *Social Theory and Social Structure*, Glencoe, Illinois: Free Press, 1957

Miles, R. *Racism and Migrant Labour*, Routledge, 1982

Millham, S, Bullock, R, Hosie, K. and Haak, M. *Lost in Care, The Problems of Maintaining Links between Children in Care and their Families*, Dartington Social Research Unit, Gower, 1986

Mills, C.W. *The Sociological Imagination*, Oxford University Press, 1959

Moser, C.A. and Kalton, G. *Survey Methods in Social Investigation*, H.E.B., 1971

Mouffe, C. *Gramsci and Marxist Thought*, Routledge and Kegan Paul, 1979

Moyser, G. and Wagstaffe, M. *The Methodology of Elite Interviewing*, Economic and Social Research Council, 1985

Mujahid quoted by McCulloch, J.W. and Kornreich, R. in 'Black People and the Social Services Departments, Problems and Perspectives', in Brown M.J. (ed) *Social Issues in the Social Services*, Charles Knight, 1974

Myrdal, G. *An American Dilemma*, Harper Bros, 1944

National Association for the Care and Resettlement of Offenders 'Black People and the Criminal Justice System' A report of one day conference held on 11 May 1985, NACRO

National Association for the Care and Resettlement of Offenders 'Black People and the Criminal Justice System', A report of the NACRO Race Issues National Advisory Committee, NACRO, 1986

National Association for the Care and Resettlement of Offenders 'Race and Criminal Justice: A Way Forward', A second report of the NACRO Race Issues National Advisory Committee, NACRO, 1989

National Children's Home 'The Problem of the Coloured Child: The Experience of the National Children's Home', Child Care Quarterly, 8(2), 1954

Neilson, J. 'Tayori: Black homes for black children', *Child Welfare*, 55, 1976, pp. 41–53

Nemeth, T. *Gramsci's Philosophy: A Critical study*, Harvester Press, 1980

OFFICE OF POPULATION CENSUSES AND SURVEYS *1981 Census of England and Wales*, HMSO, 1983

O'HIGGINS, K. and BOYLE, M. 'State Care – Some Children's Alternatives, An Analysis of the Data from the Returns to the Department of Health, Child Care Division, 1982', The Economic and Social Research Institute, 1988

OLIN, R.J. 'Program Evaluation in a Family Service Agency', *Social Casework*, Feb 1986, pp. 108–112

OPPENHEIM, A.N. *Questionnaire Design and Attitude Measurement*, H.E.B., 1968

OUSLEY, M. et al *The System*, Runnymede Trust and South London Equal Rights Consultancy Publications, 1981

PEP 'A Report on Racial Discrimination, no 544, Political and Economic Planning', 1967

PACKMAN, J. *The Child's Generation*, 2nd edn, Basil Blackwell and Martin Robertson, 1981

PACKMAN, J, RANDALL, J. and JACQUES, N. *Who Needs Care – Social Work Decisions about Children*, Basil Blackwell, 1986

PARK, R.E. 'Racial Assimilation in Secondary Groups with Particular Reference to the Negro', Publication to the American Sociological Society, 8, 1913, pp. 66–83

PARTON, N. 'The Natural History of Child Abuse: A Study in Social Problem Definition', *British Journal of Social Work*, 9(4), 19079, pp. 431–51

PARTON, N. 'Child Abuse, Social Anxiety and Welfare', *British Journal of Social Work*, 11(4), 1981, pp. 391–414

PARTON, N. 'The Beckford Report: A Critical Appraisal', *British Journal of Social Work*, 16(5), 1986, pp. 511–530

PAYNE, S. 'Long Term Placement for the Black Child in Care', Social Work Monograph 15, University of East Anglia, 1983

PEARCE, K.S. 'West Indian Boys in Community Home Schools', Unpublished Thesis for the Diploma in the Educational Rehabilitation of Young People, University of London Institute of Education, Published in Abridged form in *Community Schools Gazette*, 68(6)(7)(8), 1974

PEARSON, D.G. *Race, Class and Political Activism: A Study of West Indians in Britain*, Gower, 1981

PHILLIPS, D. and MARSH, P. 'Doing Social Work Research', *Research, Policy and Planning*, 2(2), 1984

PHILLIPS, D.L. *Knowledge From What? Theories and Methods in Social Research*, Rand McNally, 1971

PINDER, R. and SHAW, M. 'Coloured Children in Long Term Care', Unpublished Report, University of Leicester, School of Social Work, 1974

PINDER, R. 'Encountering Diversity: Observations on the Social Work Assessment of Black Children', University of Leeds, Centre for Social Work and Applied Social Studies, Occasional Paper. No 9, 1982

PLATT, J. *Realities of Social Research*, Halstead Press, 1976

POPPER, K.R. *The Logic of Scientific Discovery*, Hutchinson, 1959

POPPER, K.R. *The Poverty of Historicism*, Routledge and Kegan Paul, 1957

141

PROTTAS, J.M. 'The Power of the Street Level Bureaucrat in Public Service Bureaucracies', *Urban Affairs Quarterly*, 13 March 1978

RACISM (London: Counter Information Services, 1976) p34, quoted in SIMPKIN, M *Trapped Within Welfare*, Macmillan, 1979

RACK, P. *Race, Culture and Mental Disorder*, Tavistock, 1982

RANDALL, F. *British Social Services*, Macdonald and Evans, 1981

RATCLIFFE, P. *Racism and Reaction, A Profile of Handsworth*, Routledge and Kegan Paul, 1981

RAYNOR, L. *Adoption of Non-White Children in Britain*, Allen & Unwin, 1970

REX, J. and MOORE, R. *Race, Community and Conflict*, Oxford University Press, 1967

REX, J. and TOMLINSON, S. *Colonial Immigrants in British City: A Class Analysis*, Routledge and Kegan Paul, 1979

REX, J. *Race and Ethnicity*, Open University Press, 1986

REX, J. and MASON, D. (eds) *Theories of Race and Ethnic Relations*, University Press, 1986

RHODES, P. *Racial Matching in fostering, Aldershot: Avebury* 1992

ROGERS, C. *Counselling and Psychotherapy: Newer Concepts in Practice*, Houghton Mifflin, 1942

ROONEY, B. 'Black Social Workers in White Departments', in CHEETHAM, J. (ed) *Social Work and Ethnicity*, Allen & Unwin, 1982

ROSE, E.J.B. et al *Colour and Citizenship: A Report on British Race Relations*, Oxford University Press; 1969

ROSENBURG, M. *Society and the Adolescent Self-Image*, Princeton University Press, 1965

ROWE, J. and LAMBERT, L. *Children Who Wait*, Association of British Adoption Agencies, 1973

ROWE, J, CAIN, H, HUNDLEBY, M. and KEANE, A. *Long Term Foster Care*, Batsford/British Agencies for Adoption and Fostering, 1984

ROWE, J. HUNDLEBY, M. and GARNETT, L. *Child Care Now*, BAAF, Research Series 6, 1989

ROYS, P. 'Social Services' in BHAT, A., CARR-HILL, R. and OHRI, S. (eds) *Britain's Black Population, A New Perspective*, 2nd edn, The Radical Statistics Race Group, Gower, 1988

SALAMAN, G. and THOMPSON, K. (eds) *Control and Ideology in Organisations*, Open University Press, 1980

SAMUELS, A. 'Trans-Racial Adoption – Adoption of the Black Child', Family Law, 9(8), 1979, pp. 237–239

SATYAMURTI, C. *Occupational Survival*, Blackwell, 1981

SCHOFIELD, M. *Social Research*, (Concepts Books No.8), Heinemann, 1969

SEEBOHM REPORT 'Report of the Committee on Local Authority and Allied Personal Social Services', Cmnd 3703, HMSO, 1968

SEED, P. *The Expansion of Social Work in Britain*, Routledge and Kegan Paul, 1973

SHARDLOW, S. (ed) *The Values of Change in Social Work*, Tavistock/Routledge, 1989

SHERMAN, A 'Britain's Urge to Self-Destruction', The *Daily Telegraph*, 9 September 1979

SILLITOE, K. 'Ethnic Origin, the search for a question', *Population Trends*, 13, 1978

SILVERMAN, D. *Qualitative Methodology and Sociology*, Gower, 1985

SIMON, R. *Gramsci's Political Thought*, Lawrence and Wishart, 1982

SIMPKIN, M. *Trapped within Welfare*, Macmillan, 1983

SIMON, R.J. and ALSTEIN, H. *Transracial Adoption*, Wiley and Sons, 1977

SIMON, R.J. and ALSTEIN, H. *Transracial Adoption: A follow-up*, Lexington Books, 1981

SINCLAIR, R. *Decision Making in Statutory Reviews on Children in Care*, Gower, 1984

SIVANANDAN, A. 'Race, Class and the State', *Race and Class*, 17, Spring 1976

SIVANANDAN, A. From immigration control to induced repatriation', *Race and Class* 20(1), 1978

SIVANANDAN, A. 'Challenging Racism: Strategies for the 80s', *Race and Class*, 25(2), 1983, pp. 1–11

SMALL, J. 'The Crisis in Adoption', *International Journal of Psychiatry*, 30, Spring 1984, pp. 129–142

SMITH, D. *The Facts of Racial Disadvantage*, Political and Economic Planning, 1976

SMITH, H.W. *Strategies of Social Research*, Prentice-Hall, 1975

SMITH, N, BATTA, I, and McCULLOCH, J. 'A Comparison by Colour of Boys in a Classifying School', *Probation Journal*, 22(3), 1975, pp. 87–91

SMITH, N. and McCULLOCH, J. 'Immigrants' Knowledge and Experience Of Social Work Services', *Mental Health and Society*, 4(3-4), 1977, pp. 130–7

SOLOMOS, J. 'Varieties of Marxist Conceptions of "Race", Class and the State: A Critical Analysis', in REX, J. and MASON, J. (eds) *Theories of Race and Ethnic Relations*, Cambridge University Press, 1986

SOUL KIDS CAMPAIGN Association of British Adoption and Fostering Agencies, ABAFA, 1976

SPRIANO, P. *Antonio Gramsci and the Party, the Prison Years*, Lawrence and Wishart, 1979

STAINTON ROGERS, W. 'Childrearing in a Multicultural Society', in STAINTON ROGERS, W. and ASH, E. (eds) *Child Abuse and Neglect*, Batsford, 1989

STAPLES, R. (ed) *The Black Family: Essays and Studies*, Woodstock, 1978

STATHAM, D. *Radicals in Social Work*, Routledge and Kegan Paul, 1978

STEIN, M. and CAREY, K. *Leaving Care*, Blackwell, 1986

STEVENSON, O. 'Reception into care – its meaning for all concerned', in TOD, R. (ed) *Children in Care*, Longman, 1968

STEVENSON, O. and SMITH, J. 'The Implementation of Section 56 of the Children Act 1975', Unpublished Research Report

STONE, M. *The Education of the black child in Britain: The Myth of Multiracial Education*, Fontana, 1981

STUBBS, P. 'The Employment of Black Social Workers: From Ethnic Sensitivity to Anti-Racism', *Critical Social Policy*, 12, Spring 1985, pp. 6–27

TAYLOR, W. *Probation and After Care in a Multi-Racial Society*, CRE, 1981

THANE, P. *The Foundation of the Welfare State*, Longman, 1982

THOBURN, J. *Captive Clients*, Routledge and Kegan Paul, 1980

THOBURN, J, MURDOCH, A. and O'BRIEN, A. *Permanence in Child Care*, Basil Blackwell, 1986

TIPLER, J. 'Is Justice Colour-Blind? A Study of the Impact of Race in the Juvenile Justice System in Hackney', Social Services Research Note 6, 1986

TIZARD, B. (1977) *Adoption: A Second Chance*, Free Press, 1977

TIZARD, B. and PHOENIX, A. 'Black Identity and Transracial Adoption', *New Community*, 15(3), April 1989

TOWER HAMLET DIRECTORATE OF SOCIAL SERVICES 'Children who come into care in Tower Hamlets', London Borough of Tower Hamlets, A. Wilkinson, 1982

TOWNSEND, P. *The Last Refuge*, Routledge and Kegan Paul, 1964

TOYNBEE, P. 'Care?', The *Guardian*, 2 Dec 1985

TRISELIOTIS, J.P. (ed) *Social Work with Immigrant Clients*, Oxford University Press, 1972

VENNER, M. 'West Indian Families in Britain: A Research Note, *New Community*, 12(3), Winter 1985

VERNON, J. and FRUIN, D. *In Care – A Study of Social Work Decision Making*, National Children's Bureau, 1986

WALKER, M.A. 'The Court Disposal of Young Males, by Race, in London in 1983', *British Journal of Criminology*, 1988

WALLACE, W. 'The logic of science in sociology', 1971, in BYNNER, J. and STRIBELY, K.M. (eds) *Social Research: principles and procedures*, Open University Press, 1979

WEBB, A. and WISTOW, G. *Social Work, Social Care and Social Planning: The Personal Social Services Since Seebohm*, Longman, 1987

WEINREICH, P. 'The Operationalisation of Identity Theory in Racial and Ethnic Relations', in REX, J. and MASON, D. (eds) *Theories of Race and Ethnic Relations*, Cambridge University Press, 1986

WEISE, J. 'Transracial Adoption', Social Work Monograph 60, University of East Anglia, 1988

WILDING, P. *Professional Power and Social Welfare*, Routledge and Kegan Paul, 1982

WILKINSON, S.H.P. *Birth is more than once: The Inner World of Adopted Korean Children*, Harlo Press, Detroit, 1985

WILSON, A. 'Mixed Race Children: An Exploratory Study of Racial Categorisation and Identity', *New Community*, Spring-Summer 1981, pp. 36–43

WILSON, H. 'Parenting in Poverty', *British Journal Of Social Work*, 4(3) 1973, pp. 241–254

WILSON, M.B. 'An Evaluation of the Determinants of Positive Outcome in Child Guidance Social Work', *British Journal of Social Work*, 15, 1985, pp. 363–374

WISEMAN, J.P. 'The Research Web', in BYNNER J. and STRIBLEY, K.M. (eds) *Social Research: Principles and Procedures*, The Open University Press, 1985

# Index

**Bold** references refer to whole sections